Discourse and the Other

Discourse and the Other

The Production of the Afro-American Text

W. Lawrence Hogue

Duke University Press   Durham   1986

Library of Congress Cataloging-in-Publication Data

Hogue, W. Lawrence, 1951–
  Discourse and the other.

  Bibliography: p.
  Includes index.
    1. American literature—Afro-American authors—
History and criticism. 2. Afro-Americans—Intellectual
life. 3. Literature and society—United States.
4. Criticism—United States—History—20th century.
5. Canon (Literature) I. Title.
PS153.N5H6   1986   810'.9'896   86-13472
ISBN 0-8223-0676-X

To the Hogue and Taylor clans,
who taught me those early lessons in *style*.

Contents

Preface

Novelist and essayist Joan Didion begins the first chapter of *The White Album* by remarking, "We tell ourselves stories in order to live." Didion's statement is a paradigm in a postmodern world where individuals have come to mistrust many, if not all, of the myths, conventions, and stereotypes that were once considered "natural" and sacred. The act of telling (and writing) stories has become a way in which we attempt to establish new and relevant myths and conventions to explain our lived experiences.

This book is my attempt to produce new definitions of and assumptions about literature that complement my own political and social interests and concerns, my own lived experiences. In writing the book, I had a number of questions and concerns in mind. First, I wanted to examine how literary texts in general, and Afro-American texts in particular, are produced, defined, interpreted, and appropriated, how they function politically and culturally. I was concerned with why certain books are published and promoted, or defined as "great," and others are published and ignored. What criteria and standards are used to determine the merits of a literary text? Are these criteria and standards derived ideologically? If they are, what implications does this derivation have for literature? Second, I was concerned especially with what role editors, review journals and magazines (criticism), awarding agencies, and English departments play in the production of literary texts. What role do these institutions play in reproducing these standards and criteria?

The germ of my questions and concerns developed in undergraduate school where I found certain assumptions about literature and certain critical practices incongruent with my own political and critical questions—especially those questions that deal with the relation between literature and society. Many of these questions were examined thoroughly when I was a graduate student in the Program in Modern Thought and Literature at Stanford University. A number of professors and colleagues at Stanford assisted me with this examination. To them, I want to express my deepest appreciation. First, for their assistance, encouragement, and guidance, I want to express thanks to: Professor David Halliburton, my principal dissertation advisor, for introducing me to critical theory, for his unselfish guidance and direction, and for believing in me during those formative years; Professor William Mills Todd III for his exactness in all things, for his sharp insights, for his honest interest and energetic encouragement, and for reading and offering invaluable suggestions on an earlier draft of this book; Professor Sylvia Wynter for her challenging and encouraging interchanges in the "corridors" and for convincing me that critical theory has a place in Afro-American studies. I would also like to thank Clyde Taylor for long and at times intense dialogues about Afro-American literature and the future of Afro-American critical practice.

I want to thank Glenn Jordan, whom I met as a graduate student at Stanford, for being not only an interested and driving colleague but also a friend. Glenn Jordan encouraged me to write about the sacreds and to explain the silences. I want to thank Professor Aliko Songolo of the UCI French department for his support and guidance as I went about the business of teaching and writing at the University of California, Irvine. Thanks also goes to Professor Wilfred Samuels, a postdoctoral colleague in the Center for Afro-American Studies at the University of California, Los Angeles, and a professor of English at Prairie View A&M University in Texas, for his support and encouragement and for reading the book and offering invaluable comments and suggestions. A special thanks to Professor Garrett Hongo of the English department of the University of Missouri, Columbia, who, through dialogues and conversations, assisted me in working through some theoretical concepts—especially as they apply to the defined Other, minorities, in the United States. I wish to thank Professor Cornel West of Yale University's philosophy department, whose wealth of knowledge and close reading of the book allowed me to clarify, expand, and add certain crucial arguments. A special thanks to my colleague Professor Michael Clark of the University of California, Irvine, whose Foucauldian insights helped me shape this final draft. Finally, I wish to thank Erskine Peters of the University of California, Berkeley; Ronald Johnson; and Douglass Davidson of the University of Illinois, Urbana, for reading portions of the book and offering suggestions and comments.

The research and writing of this book have also benefited from the generous assistance and support of several organizations and institutions. I want to thank the University of California, Irvine, for a faculty development grant (fall 1981) that relieved me of a quarter of my teaching responsibilities to work full-time on the book. I wish to thank the National Research Council for a Ford Foundation Fellowship (1982–83) that gave me a year's leave to complete most of the writing of this book. With warmest appreciation I thank director Claudia Mitchell-Kernan and the Center for Afro-American Studies at the University of California, Los Angeles, for my tenure as a visiting research scholar (1982–83), for opening up all the services of the center, for making the enormous resources within the university available, and for providing me with an interdisciplinary intellectual ambience in which to conduct my research and writing. I thank Professor Ken Bailes, dean of humanities at the University of California, Irvine, for 1983 and 1984 summer grants to continue working on the book. I wish to thank Jane Bitar and the staff of the Word Processing Service Center at UCLA (especially Michael Chandler for his patience with the revisions) for their efficiency and proficiency in getting this book in legible form. I want to thank Joanne Ferguson, editor-in-chief and assistant director of Duke University Press, who recognized the critical worth of this book and saw it through to publication. Last, I want to thank the members of the Hogue and Taylor clans who through telephone calls, letters, and visits allowed me to know that this one is for the family.

Discourse and the Other

Chapter 1. Literary Production:
A Silence in Afro-American Critical Practice

Recent advances in modern linguistics, along with developments in semiotics and Michel Foucault's concept of discursive formations, have eroded many of the assumptions and presuppositions traditionally associated with literature and criticism. This erosion has proven fundamental. Literary modes and categories inherited from the past no longer accommodate the concerns and questions posed by a new generation of literary scholars and intellectuals. The traditional concept of realism has been proven inadequate. The proposition that the writer is the "creator" of something "original" has come under serious attack. The unquestioned assumption of the text's literariness—that is, that the text possesses certain qualities that place it above the matrices of historical conditions—has been undermined profoundly. Definitions of artistic beauty, greatness in literary texts, and literary worth and value have been deemed subjective and ideological. The conjecture that the writer writes to tell the "truth" has been denounced vehemently. Last, the once acceptable assumptions that critical practice is an innocent activity and that the literary text is inextricably owned by and exclusively associated with the discipline of "literature" have been quelled almost completely.

Developments in semiotics and Foucault's concept of discursive formations produce the theoretical space that allows the literary critic to shift criticism's concerns and focus from a juridical to a theoretical status. In traditional or normative critical practices, the text is subordinated to what Pierre Macherey calls an "external principle of legality," an "aesthetic legality [that] has a juridical rather than a theoretical status; . . . its rules merely restrain the writer's activity. Because it is powerless to examine the work on its own terms. . . , [normative] criticism resorts to a corroding resentment."[1] In its theoretical status, critical practice is a certain "form of knowledge" which has a particular condition for its existence.

Further, these developments allow the formation of critical practices that shift criticism's focus from the world of creation, the scene of charismatic authorship, to a specific productive process, a set of operations that transform a given language into something new. The literary text becomes not a tangible object that can be held in hand, but a textual system that transposes one or more systems of sign into another. This textual system is composed of a dispersion of its statements and its gaps and silences. The fact that the text permits and excludes certain statements exposes its exclusionary judgments and shows how it functions as a cultural object with social impact that can be calculated politically.

These advancements and developments have produced the critical and theoretical options for Afro-American and other minority texts, and for self-conscious and avant-garde texts—texts whose formations are different from or exist outside established definitions of the literary experience—to be assessed and explained. They give this new generation of literary critics and scholars the theoretical option to ask new questions of the literary text, to examine its mode of production. They also give the critical option to reexamine and reassess those American texts that have been deemed "great" by institutions such as review journals and magazines, English departments, editors, and granting and awarding agencies within the ruling cultural apparatus.

In any literate society there exist a number of distinct modes of literary production that Terry Eagleton defines as "a unity of certain forces and social relations of literary production."[2] Most literary productions belong to the dominant formation's cultural apparatus, which includes the specific institutions of literary production and distribution—editors, publishing houses, bookstores, and libraries. The cultural apparatus also encompasses a range of secondary supporting institutions—among them literary academies, English departments, literary criticism, the concept of literature, granting and awarding agencies—whose function is more directly ideological. These secondary supportive institutions are concerned with the definition and dissemination of certain codified literary standards, conventions, stereotypes, and assumptions.

The concept of literature, produced historically and ideologically, generates these established literary conventions, stereotypes, and assumptions. The current definition of literature began taking shape during the latter half of the eighteenth century. With a Latin root, *littera,* literature was, in effect, a condition of reading: of being able to read and of having read. It was close to the modern sense of literacy.

In its modern form, however, literature has come to mean, as Raymond Williams notes, "taste," "sensibility," and "discrimination."[3] These terms become the unifying concepts of modern literature. They comprise a practice that produces the organization into which forms of imaginative writing are compressed. These forms reflect a historically and ideologically produced way of viewing literary texts. In short, literature becomes a construction "fashioned by particular people for particular reasons."[4]

Editors, publishers, critics, and reviewers function as a kind of conduit for many of the established cultural, ideological, and intellectual preferences. They are instrumental in keeping certain ideas, social habits, myths, moral conventions, and stereotypes alive in the public's mind—usually under the pretext of not wanting to upset the status quo or offend the public. These editors and critics seek their own definitions of the literary experience in all texts that come to their attention. They evaluate texts by pointing out their contribution to "knowledge" and by explaining how they reproduce certain values, conventions, stereotypes, and perspectives. They certify those literary texts that speak the discourse better, that conform to the established literary standards and criteria. They exclude those texts that do not conform in subject or perspective, on the grounds that they are inferior aesthetically—thereby effecting certain silences in the discourse of literature.

My intention is not to put forth the simplistic argument that the only literary texts published are those that reproduce mainstream literary conventions, values, and stereotypes. English departments, literary journals and magazines, editors, and publishers often espouse values and meanings that are antithetical to those of mainstream society. But these antithetical values and meanings are compatible with specific forms of discourse that allow them to be appropriated. They either speak a particular language or accept a particular form that will not permit certain meanings and positions to be articulated.[5]

Publishers, in particular, play a crucial role in reproducing established literary conventions and stereotypes by catering to the normative, hypothesized reader. In *The Sociology of Literature,* Robert Escarpit contends that with the rise of the middle class in eighteenth-century England, literature ceased to be the privilege of men of letters.[6] It shifted its focus and concerns from the aristocracy to the bourgeoisie who demanded a literature that suited their own concerns, that reproduced their values.

With this large middle-class audience the publisher found himself, and still does, caught between the writer's desire and the public's demands. To accommodate, the publisher influences his writer in the interest of the public by giving advances for the production of particular kinds of books. He influences the public through censoring and advertising in the interest of the writer. In short, the publisher induces a compatible writer-public relationship. But, as Maria Corti explains, the publisher fails to make a distinction between the "effective, virtual reader" and the "hypothesized reader."[7]

A consequence of the publisher's appeal to the mass "hypothesized reader" is that marginal and "other" groups are not seen as constituting a real audience. This oversight contributes to the weeding out or exclusion of certain literary texts. This induced writer-public relationship also coerces some writers with nonconformist perspectives and values into writing for the "hypothesized reader." When a writer is forced to write for an alien reader, Robert Escarpit points out, a "sort of detachment results which may allow the author to have an ideology different from that of his readers and to have to decide on the meaning not only of his own work, but of literature itself."[8]

Criticism as practiced by editors, publishers, reviewers, and critics, then, is not scientific; it is a preeminently political exercise that works upon and mediates the reception of literary texts. It is an active and ongoing part of literature and the cultural apparatus as they produce objects whose "effects" function to reproduce a particular literary experience, or particular literary conventions and stereotypes. As a series of interventions within the uses to which so-called literary texts are to be put, critical practice sends out signals as to the worth and value of literary texts. Those literary texts that reproduce particular literary "experiences" are promoted and certified. Those that do not reproduce certain "experiences" or ideological effects are repressed or subordinated.

Perhaps a discussion of Michel Foucault's concepts of discourse and discursive formations can facilitate an understanding of how critical practice and the concept of literature exclude certain forms of literature, and how critical practice's assumptions, represented as value judgments or as "natural" criteria, actually operate within a network of discursive regulations that finally include the broadest ideological constraints and practices.

For Michel Foucault, a discourse is *any* group of statements that exists under the positive condition of a complex group of relations. He calls this group of relations *discursive.* The regularity that binds the object's relations he calls *discursive formation.*[9] A discursive formation does not connect concepts or words with one another. Instead, it offers concepts the objects of which they can speak. It determines the group of relations that a discourse must establish before it can speak of a particular object. These relations characterize not the language used by discourse but discourse itself as a practice. The conditions to which the group of relations are subjected Foucault calls the *rules of formation.*[10]

Within a discourse exist relations of mutual delimitation. The whole group of relations forms a principle of determination that permits and excludes a certain number of statements. This means that a discourse does not occupy all the possible space that is open to it by the mere nature of its system of formation.

It is essentially incomplete. The incompleteness is manifested in gaps, silences, discontinuities, and limitations.

But discourse conceals its incompleteness, its mode of formation. It naturalizes itself by inscribing its discursive practice in its method of category selection. For Foucault, the archaeologist's function is to demask this process of naturalization, to expose the various ways in which discourse, or any form of representation, deludes. In inserting this signifying process into the social process, we can see not just how literary texts, canons, standards, myths, and conventions are produced, but also how culture, as well, is produced or invented, rather than being "natural," absolute, or eternal.

Without demasking this process of naturalization, a "natural" or mainstream definition of the literary "experience" will continue to universalize the ideological and historical forces that produced it. Its agents will continue to assume that literature reflects or mirrors the social reality rather than being a production of it. They will continue to assume that "universal" standards exist to measure the literary text's value and worth, rather than seeing its worth as determined within a cultural or ideological context.

For almost a century, Afro-American critics and writers have been aware of the ways in which ideological pressures have dictated the canon of American literature. They also have been aware of the exclusion of certain Afro-American literary texts, images, and conventions from that canon. If we read the letters and fiction of the nineteenth-century writer Charles Chesnutt, which will be discussed in detail in the next chapter, we can discern clearly his awareness that certain literary images, stereotypes, and conventions are sanctioned and promoted by editors, publishers, and critics, and that other Afro-American images and stereotypes are repressed or subordinated. If we read the essays of Zora Neale Hurston almost fifty years later, we again can discern that she too was quite aware of the pressures by ruling literary institutions to prohibit certain Afro-American images and texts. Recently, Mary Helen Washington in *Black-Eyed Susans,* Barbara Smith in *Home Girls: A Black Feminist Anthology* and in *Some of Us Are Brave,* and others have continued to document the exclusion of blacks and women from the established literary practices in America.

But Chesnutt, Hurston, Washington, Smith, and Afro-American critics of the twentieth century have not examined conceptually the discursive nature of exclusion either in American literature, or in Afro-American and women's literatures. Most Afro-American critical practices, which are my concern here, do not engage their own productive process. They universalize the ideological and historical forces that produce them. They are also silent on the production of Afro-American texts. These critical practices ignore the various literary and ideological forces that actually cause certain Afro-American texts to be published, promoted, and certified and others to be subordinated and/or excluded. They ignore the historically and ideologically established way of viewing literary texts and how this established way affects the production of Afro-American literary texts.

In an article entitled "Generational Shifts and the Recent Criticism of Afro-American Literature," Houston A. Baker, Jr., delineates three dominant critical practices that have defined Afro-American literature in the past forty years. Baker argues that "poetics of integration" defined Afro-American literature during the 1940s and 1950s. The assumptions and criteria for this practice, for defining Afro-American literature, were established by Arthur P. Davis and reached their maturity with Richard Wright. In the introduction to *The Negro Caravan* (1941), Davis writes:

> The editors . . . do not believe that the expression "Negro Literature" is an accurate one, and in spite of its convenient brevity, they have avoided using it. "Negro Literature" has no application if it means *structural peculiarity,* or a Negro school of writing. The Negro writes in the forms evolved in English and American literature. . . . The editors consider Negro writers to be American writers, and literature by American Negroes to be a segment of American literature.[11]

Davis reiterates this integrationist critical practice in his essay, "Integration and Race Literature," which, as Baker informs us,

he presented to the first conference on Afro-American writers
sponsored by the American society of African Culture in 1959.
Here Davis explains, "The integration controversy is another crisis, and from it we hope that the Negro will move permanently
into full participation of American life—social, economic, political, and literary."[12]

In his essay "The Literature of the Negro in the United
States," published in 1957, Richard Wright viewed the Supreme
Court case of *Brown v. Board of Education* as the beginning of
the end of racial discrimination in the United States. Wright believed that Afro-American literature would become indistinguish-
able from the literature of the dominant American society: "At
the present moment there is no one dominant note in Negro literary expression. As the Negro merges into the mainstream of
American life, there might result actually a disappearance of
Negro as such."[13] In the 1950s this "poetics of integration" oper-
ated within a network of discursive regulations that included the
broadest ideological constraints and practices. It was a part of a
dominant assimilationist ideological base—in many instances
sanctioned by the dominant American cultural apparatus—
whose practices were reproduced in Afro-American cultural, political, and literary arenas.

As major Afro-American writers and critics in the 1940s and
1950s, Wright and Davis were able, through their anthologies,
reviews, criticisms, and status within the literary world, to establish a tradition and promote a body of Afro-American literature
that reflected the values, conventions, and stereotypes of their
integrationist perspective on literary texts. For example, during
the 1940s and 1950s when Gwendolyn Brooks was writing
"mainstream" poetry, Wright was instrumental in getting her
work published by Harper and Row.[14]

Arthur P. Davis in his many anthologies also promoted a particular kind of integrationist Afro-American literature. For example, in *From the Dark Tower: Afro-American Writers 1900–1960,*
Davis states that a "major Negro writer is one whose work deals
largely with the black experience, measures up to appropriate
aesthetic standards, and influences to some extent his contempo-
raries and/or those who come after."[15] For Davis, "appropriate

aesthetic standards" are those standards sanctioned by the dominant American literary establishment. Discussing Paul Laurence
Dunbar and Charles Chesnutt, Davis implies that they are
"major" Negro writers because both "appeared in America's best
periodicals of the age, and both had their works produced by the
finest publishing houses."[16]

Davis includes Richard Wright, Chester Himes, Ann Petry,
and Julian Mayfield in his section on "Toward the Mainstream"
as "major" Negro writers because their naturalist works had the
"message of protest against America's treatment of its black minority."[17] Their works have the "spiritual commitment and climate out of which full integration could develop."[18] Owen
Dodson's *Boy at the Window* and Gwendolyn Brooks's *Maud
Martha* are considered minor works and therefore are excluded
because they give "intimate and subtle vignettes of middle class
living."

But this integrationist way of viewing Afro-American literary
texts, by the mere nature of its concerns, excluded other perspectives (in the next chapter, see Wright's treatment of Hurston's
Their Eyes Were Watching God). With strong-willed determination to "merge into the mainstream of American life," to write
"in the forms evolved in English and American literature," both
Wright and Davis accept as "natural" the mainstream literary assumptions about literature. They assume that English and American literature has standards and criteria which Afro-American
writers must reproduce if they are to write "good" literature. In
not interpreting these fundamental assumptions as a function of
some broader ideological practice, or as belonging to a literary
discourse that permits and excludes certain literary texts, both
Davis and Wright ignore the literary and ideological forces that
produce Afro-American literature. In addition, they ignore how
their own critical practice is the product of exclusionary judgments and how it therefore defines an Afro-American tradition
that appropriates certain Afro-American texts and excludes others.

In his essay "Generational Shifts and the Recent Criticism of
Afro-American Literature," Baker further contends that a group
of Afro-American writers, intellectuals, and critics—who had a
different ideological disposition toward American egalitarianism

than those who espoused poetics of integration—emerged in the 1960s: "The emerging generation sets itself the task of analyzing the nature, aims, ends, and arts of those hundreds of thousands of their own people who were assaulting America's manifest structures of exclusion."[19] The critical practice that accompanied this new ideological shift within the Afro-American political arena was one of cultural nationalism, which has its own "structures of exclusion." This nationalist critical practice has its origins in Langston Hughes's writing in the 1920s and its culmination in Amiri Baraka's cultural nationalism of the 1960s and Addison Gayle's black aesthetic of the 1970s. In discussing who will become the "great Negro artist" and what his subject will be, Hughes writes:

> But then there are the low-down folks, the so-called common element, and they are the majority—may the Lord be praised! The people who have their nip of gin on Saturday nights are not too important to themselves . . . to watch the lazy world go round. They . . . do not particularly care whether they are like white folks or anybody else. Their joy runs, bang! into ecstasy. Their religion soars to a shout. Work maybe a little today, rest a little tomorrow. Play a while. Sing a while. O, let's dance. These common people are not afraid of spirituals. . . . They furnish a wealth of colorful, distinctive material for any artist because they still hold their own individuality in the face of American standardizations. And perhaps these common people will give to the world its truly great Negro artist, the one who is not afraid to be himself.[20]

Hughes's advocacy of an Afro-American literature emphasizing "the common people" who "do not care whether they are like white folks," who still "hold their own individuality in the face of American standardizations," is echoed in the cultural nationalism of Amiri Baraka in the 1960s:

> Where is the Negro-ness of a literature written in imitation of the meanest of social intelligences to be found in American culture, i.e., the white middle class? How can it even begin to express the emotional predicament of black western man?

Such a literature, even if its "characters *are* black, takes on the emotional barrenness of its model, and the blackness of the characters is like the blackness of Al Jolson, an unconvincing device. It is like using black checkers instead of white. They [are] still checkers.[21]

Hughes's and Baraka's advocacy of a nationalist Afro-American literature culminated in the black arts movement of the 1960s and in the black aesthetic critical practice of the late sixties and early seventies whose leading exponents included Ron Karenga, Holt Fuller, and Addison Gayle. These black aestheticians—through their critical texts and major Afro-American review journals and magazines like *Black World, First World, Black Books Bulletin, The Black Scholar*—define Afro-American literature along cultural nationalist criteria. They define the worth of Afro-American literary texts according to how accurately these texts reproduce the cultural nationalist's ideologically defined Afro-American historical experience. These black aestheticians seek their meaning of the Afro-American experience in all Afro-American texts that come to their attention—praising those that reproduce their values, conventions, and stereotypes and condemning those that do not. In *The Way of the New World: The Black Novel in America,* Addison Gayle, using the black aesthetic criteria, determines the worth and value of Afro-American texts from William Wells Brown's *Clotel, or The President's Daughter* (1853) to Ernest J. Gaines's *The Autobiography of Miss Jane Pittman* (1971). Gayle praises those texts—like Delany's *Blake,* Chesnutt's *The Marrow of Tradition,* McKay's *Banana Bottom* and *Home to Harlem,* Killens's *And Then We Heard the Thunder,* and Gaines's *Miss Jane Pittman*—that reproduce stereotypes, conventions, and values from the Afro-American experience of the cultural nationalist world view.

These black aestheticians also exclude those Afro-American texts that do not reproduce the values and conventions of their world view. In *The Way of the New World,* Gayle criticizes texts such as Johnson's *The Autobiography of an Ex-Coloured Man,* Wright's *Native Son,* and Ellison's *Invisible Man,* that use mainstream conventions and stereotypes such as alienation, existentialism, and naturalism to define the Afro-American. In using literature to further their political ends, Gayle and other black aestheticians understand the political function of literature. They know that it implies a particular form of politics, that all literary theories presuppose a certain use of literature. They understand that literature is a social institution that functions to keep certain cultural forms, values, and myths before the reading public. Their strategy is to promote those Afro-American texts that present their preferred myths and cultural forms. But this black aesthetic theory of literature is silent completely on how established literary institutions and apparatuses, throughout American literary history, have affected the production of Afro-American literature. Missing is a discussion of the various literary and ideological forces and institutions that promote those Afro-American texts that reproduce the literary values, conventions, and stereotypes of the dominant literary establishment and exclude and subordinate others. In being silent on literary production, Gayle and other black aestheticians cannot explain why certain Afro-American images and paradigms are promoted and others excluded. They cannot explain how literature is a social institution which reproduces certain codified values, conventions, or world views—be they mainstream American or black cultural nationalist. Of course, such a discussion would cause these black aestheticians to confront openly the ideological nature and function, and therefore the constraints and exclusions, of their own cultural nationalist critical practice.

In the late 1970s two Afro-American critical texts—Robert Stepto's *From Behind the Veil: A Study of Afro-American Narrative* and Houston A. Baker's *The Journey Back: Issues in Black Literature and Criticism*—established new critical perspectives for defining Afro-American literary traditions and canons. They are also silent on literary production. Stepto's *From Behind the Veil* is a "history or fiction of the historical consciousness of an Afro-American art form—namely, the Afro-American written narrative."[22] It works from three fundamental assumptions. First, Stepto assumes that Afro-American culture has its own store of "pregeneric myths" which are "shared stories or myths that not only exist prior to literary form, but eventually shape the forms that comprise a given culture's literary canon."[23] For Stepto, the primary Afro-American pregeneric myth is the "quest for freedom and literacy." Second, he assumes that once the pregeneric myth is in search of its literary forms, the Afro-American critic must "attempt to define and discuss how the myth both assumes and does not assume the properties of genre."[24] Third, Stepto assumes that if an Afro-American literary tradition does exist, it exists not because there is a "sizeable chronology of [Afro-American] authors and texts," but because these Afro-American authors and texts "collectively seek their own literary forms . . . bound historically and linguistically to a shared pregeneric myth."[25]

In *From Behind the Veil*'s first section, Stepto delineates four types of slave narratives—the eclectic, the integrated, the generic, and the authenticating. This section ends by describing how Booker T. Washington's *Up from Slavery* and W. E. B. DuBois's *The Souls of Black Folk* reproduce the generic and authenticating slave narratives. In the book's second section, Stepto demonstrates how certain "major" contemporary Afro-American narratives reproduce the types of narrative discussed in the first sections. Johnson's *The Autobiography of an Ex-Coloured Man,* Stepto argues, reproduces the generic and authenticating narratives of Washington and DuBois. Richard Wright's *Black Boy* reproduces Frederic Douglass's *Narrative,* and Ellison's *Invisible Man* reproduces both Washington's and Douglass's. Stepto isolates an Afro-American cultural myth, the pregeneric myth, and uses it to define an Afro-American literary tradition.

From Behind the Veil is valuable for a number of reasons. First, as Stepto points out in the preface, it is different or innovative because it avoids "writing yet another survey of Afro-American literature that systematically moves from texts to non-literary structures and passively allows those structures to become the literature's collective history."[26] Second, *From Behind the Veil* is valuable because it frees Afro-American texts from the matrix of dominant American critical practices, from the dominant Western historical and ideological way of defining literary texts. The book places certain Afro-American texts in an

Afro-American matrix which supports their ideological assumptions. Like the black aestheticians, Stepto understands that a literary text's value and worth are determined within a particular cultural context.

Unlike these black aestheticians, however, Stepto does not understand that all literary theories imply a particular form of politics or presuppose a certain use of literature. The mere fact that Stepto selects the "search for freedom and literacy" rather than another Afro-American myth, such as communal struggle, indicates that the choice is ideological, that his Afro-American tradition in *From Behind the Veil* is a discourse that permits and excludes. In not exposing his motives for selecting the pregeneric myth and in not informing the reader that the pregeneric myth is one of many Afro-American myths, Stepto deludes the reader into believing that the "search for freedom and literacy" is *the* pregeneric myth, is a "collective history," and that all Afro-American writers share it.

Making salient *From Behind the Veil*'s attempt to conceal its mode of production prompts the reader to ask other questions about the book. What is its cultural and ideological function? What is the relationship between Stepto's pregeneric myth and certain dominant American literary myths? What is the relationship between the dominant literary way of viewing literary texts and Stepto's way of viewing Afro-American written narratives? If we examine the "major" Afro-American written narratives that Stepto uses to establish the Afro-American pregeneric canon, we see that these narratives reproduce established American literary conventions and values. Booker T. Washington's *Up from Slavery* reproduces the dominant myth of the Protestant work ethic, for example, while Wright's *Black Boy,* Johnson's *The Autobiography of an Ex-Coloured Man,* and Ellison's *Invisible Man* chronicle the American myth of the rugged individual's quest for freedom.

This means that *From Behind the Veil* promotes those Afro-American texts that reproduce mainstream American literary myths and values. It also means that it excludes, represses, or subordinates those Afro-American texts—such as Delany's *Blake,* Bontemps's *Black Thunder,* Zora Neale Hurston's *Their*

Eyes Were Watching God, or Reed's *Mumbo Jumbo*—that do
not reproduce mainstream American literary myths and conventions. In its silence on literary production, *From Behind the Veil*
deludes the reader into believing that the Afro-American
pregeneric literary canon it produces, and the Afro-American images and representations the canon's selected texts present, reflect the Afro-American social reality. Of course, a discussion of
literary production would force Stepto to become aware of his
own ideological and cultural function as he produces a "natural"
myth about Afro-American literary texts.

Houston A. Baker, in *The Journey Back,* like Stepto identifies
myths and linguistic structures from the Afro-American historical past and uses them to construct a theory of the Afro-
American literary tradition. But like Stepto he also ignores the
fact that Afro-American myths, stereotypes, and cultural forms
are not innocent, that they are bound culturally and historically
—even within the Afro-American social reality—and therefore
have political and ideological functions.

In *The Journey Back,* Baker examines how black narrative
texts written in English "preserve and communicate culturally
unique meanings."[27] First, he describes the place occupied by
works of black literature in black American culture, and second,
he delineates how writers such as Hammon, Wheatley, Vassa,
the slave autobiographer, Wright, Ellison, Baldwin, Baraka, and
Brooks "journey through difficult straits" and in the process preserve in language details of their "voyages": "Through his [the
black writer's] work we are allowed to witness, if not the trip itself, at least a representation of the voyage that provides some
view of our emergence."[28] As with Stepto's work, the value of
Baker's *The Journey Back* lies in the fact that it understands
that a literary text's value and worth are determined within a
particular cultural context. *The Journey Back* turns to an
Afro-American cultural context to establish criteria for
interpreting and determining the worth and value of Afro-
American texts.

But in failing to deal with language as being culturally biased,
with the production of these cultural forms, and with each black
writer's "representation of the voyage" as production, Baker

neglects to reveal the force of meaning of a culture and its literature. First, in arguing that Afro-American writers can preserve in language the Afro-American historical past, Baker assumes that language reflects the social reality. But language is socially and historically produced; it is saturated with cultural and historical codes. In *Selected Writings in Language, Culture, and Personality,* Edward Sapir points out:

> Human beings do not live in the objective world alone, nor
> alone in the world of social activity as ordinarily understood,
> but are very much at the mercy of the particular language
> which has become the medium of expression for their society.
> It is quite an illusion to imagine that one adjusts to reality es-
> sentially without the use of language. . . . The fact of the mat-
> ter is that the "real world" is to a large extent unconsciously
> built upon the language habits of the group.[29]

To assume that language is transparent is to ignore the role language plays in understanding people, social history, culture, and the laws of how a society functions.

Second, in assuming that the black writer's "journey back" and his "representation of the voyage" are a reflection of the Afro-American historical past, Baker falls into an antiquated and heavily critiqued realism. According to realism, reading assumes a crossing from expression to the self, from representation to the world, from words to things, and from language to reality. But in light of the fact that modern linguistics has informed us that language is not transparent and that Foucault has informed us that all discourses, including literary texts, permit and exclude, it becomes difficult to accept Baker's supposition that the writer's "journey back" mirrors the Afro-American social reality. Instead, the "journey back" is a production of the Afro-American social reality.

Furthermore, Baker's "anthropology of art" ignores not only the writer himself or herself, but also his or her awarenesses—be they political, racial, or sexual—and how these awarenesses affect the writer's production of the "trips" and "voyages" into the past. But, more important, Baker's "anthropology of art" is silent on literary production. It ignores the role of the institutions

within the dominant cultural apparatus, as well that of Afro-
American critical practices, in producing Afro-American texts
and determining the shape of Afro-American literature. Therefore it is not surprising that he chooses Hammon, Wheatley, and
Vassa—who reproduce many of the accepted social and literary
conventions, stereotypes, and myths about the Afro-American—
to represent Afro-American literature in the eighteenth century.
Baker explains "On a first view, 'acculturation' seems to explain
everything: Hammon's progress toward Christian orthodoxy,
Wheatley's engagement with the God and muses of her white
overlords, Vassa's detailing . . . of his education as a gentle-
man."[30] If Baker's "anthropology of art" included a discussion of
literary production, it would allow him to raise questions about
those aborted and repressed Afro-American texts that do not
give acculturationist representations of the Afro-American in the
eighteenth century.

   This critique of Stepto and Baker, who identify and naturalize
certain Afro-American myths and linguistic structures, can serve
as a model for understanding the silences, limitations, and possibilities of other Afro-American critical studies in canonical formation. In the past ten years, black women scholars and writers
have worked intensely for canon formation of black women's literature. Through interviews with black women writers and
through scholarly endeavors they have identified cultural patterns and forms, perspectives, subjects, and values that are
unique or peculiar to black women writers. Barbara Christian's
*Black Women Novelists: The Development of a Tradition, 1892–
1976* is a seminal work in black women writers' canon formation. In delineating "recurrent" themes and images in the fiction
of black women novelists from Francis Harper's *Iola LeRoy*
(1892) to Alice Walker's *Meridian* (1976), Christian establishes a
tradition in novels by black women. In the first three historical
chapters Christian traces the development of dominant recurring
Afro-American stereotypes and images—the mammy, the mulatto, the wench, violent relationships between mother and father,
continuity between generations, and insularity—and the impact
they had on the production of American and black women's fiction. The next three chapters in *Black Women Novelists* are

devoted to the novels of Paule Marshall, Toni Morrison, and Alice Walker who each have "written two novels" and are "in the process of developing" their own critical visions.[31] The three novelists, Christian argues, are "very much a part of the tradition" that preceded them, but are also "developing it in some critical way."[32] In the final chapter Christian looks at the "whole tradition" and tries to "draw some conclusions about its major characteristics and about what directions it may be moving."[33]

In *Black Women Novelists,* Christian executes her intention profoundly. Like Baker and Stepto, she establishes a tradition to interpret black women writers. It is a tradition that comes from black women writers. In establishing this tradition, Christian gives us an Afro-American historical framework to use in understanding certain issues pertinent to black women, and in seeing how black women writers have textualized these issues.

But certain developments in literary theory have forced us to ask additional, or different, questions about the literary text. These new questions give us the critical space to assess the discursive aspects of Christian's critical practice. As I stated earlier, many of the traditional literary assumptions that supported literature and criticism in their traditional forms have eroded. Since the text does not reflect the social reality, what is its need or function? What are the ideological and literary forces that produce the literary text? Why is a particular text published and promoted, another published and excluded, and still another never published?

In *Black Women Novelists* Barbara Christian is quite conscious of some of these questions. She reminds her reader constantly that the literary text does not reflect the social reality. When she is discussing the Afro-American social reality produced in Harper's *Iola LeRoy,* she acknowledges that there is a "discrepancy between the substance of her novel and Harper's detailed observations of the life most black women were leading in the period of Reconstruction, a discrepancy that has something to do with the form of the novel at that time and the image of black women in American society."[34] This means that Christian is aware of certain ideological and literary forces that produce the "image of black women in American society." When

Christian writes about the communities described in the works of Marshall, Morrison, and Walker, she points out that she is "not equating the communities these authors present with the Black community. . . . The communities these authors present are more particular."[35] In addition, without revealing a clearly defined discursive formation that produces the book, Christian makes it clear that *Black Women Novelists* is "not intended to be a definitive work. I am not commenting on every black woman who has ever written a novel."[36]

Yet despite this awareness Christian's critical practice tends to lapse into normative criticism, which assumes that there is some "universal" model in social reality that can be used to measure the accuracy of the literary text. Though Christian makes it clear that there is a discrepancy between the social reality described in Harper's novel and the social reality within which she lived and wrote, she gives no insights into *Iola LeRoy* as a production, and does not explain how it "comes to be what it is because of the specific determinations of its mode of production."[37] Without discussing the issue of literary production, Christian's critical practice cannot explain fully how images of black women are tied inextricably to the production of literary texts, or why certain black women novelists are published and promoted, others published and excluded, and still others aborted at editors' and publishers' desks.

Second, despite her awareness that images of black women in fiction are incongruent with those in the social reality, Christian's critical practice lapses at times into antiquated realism. In her opinion, a "problem with Fauset's novels is that [Fauset] gives us this particular Negro [a light-complexioned, upper-middle-class black heroine] exclusively and as the representative of what the race is capable of doing."[38] But for Fauset's heroine to be "representative" of the race is to assume that literature mirrors the social reality. Fauset's novels are not representations of the social real but productions of it. The crucial question should be what are the literary and ideological forces, the "specific determinations" of their modes of production, that cause Fauset's novels to reproduce this image of the "Negro exclusively"? Whom does this produced image serve?

Third, because she does not discuss literary production, Christian cannot discuss the political and cultural significance of certain dominant American and Afro-American literary conventions and stereotypes. Although Christian informs us that the communities produced by Marshall, Morrison, and Walker do not reflect the "Black community," she never gives us insight into these writers' "communities" as produced myths or cultural objects.

Last, in chapters four through six, Christian discusses the works of Marshall, Morrison, and Walker to show how they reproduce already delineated themes and issues. Christian's argument for choosing these three novelists is that "each has written two novels and is in the process of developing her own critical vision." But one other contemporary black woman novelist, Kristin Hunter, has written three novels. Why is she excluded from Christian's tradition? Here, as with Baker and Stepto, we see how canon formation is informed by an external ideological discourse. Moreover, unless critics inform their readers of the political ramifications of their ideological discourse—as Christian attempts to do in *Black Women Novelists*—they will delude readers into believing that the tradition they espouse and the texts they select to generate that tradition really constitute the black women tradition or the Afro-American tradition.

Other anthologies and critical texts—*Sturdy Black Bridges: Visions of Black Women in Literature* (edited by Roseann P. Bell et al.), Mary Helen Washington's *Black-eyed Susans* and *Midnight Birds,* Amiri Baraka's *Confirmation,* Barbara Smith's *Some Are Brave,* Claudia Tate's *Black Women Writers at Work,* and Mari Evans's *Black Women Writers: A Critical Evaluation*—continue the examination of black women writers ferreting out traditions. But as in the cases of Stepto and Baker, these interviews and critical studies of black women writers first assume that all black women writers share the same ideological concerns about black women experience or culture. In this assumption, certain black women writers like Kristin Hunter and Pauline Hopkins who do not reproduce the prevailing women's "themes" and "issues" are subordinated or excluded. Hunter and Hopkins do not deal in their fiction with feminist categories such as black

women's historical oppression, the brutal and violent relationships between black men and black women, and black women's
sexual awareness. Consequently, they do not fit comfortably into
feminist canon formation that organizes black women's texts
around these issues.

Second, these interviews and critical studies exclude a discussion of the literary and ideological forces that have given shape,
and continue to give shape, to a body of literature called black
women's literature. Without a discussion of literary production,
these critical studies are not able to explain why certain black
women writers are published and promoted and others published
and ignored. Are certain black women writers published and
promoted because they reproduce established American literary
myths and conventions? Are other black women writers published and promoted because they reproduce certain sanctioned
Afro-American stereotypes and conventions? Are others published and ignored because they fail to reproduce sanctioned literary myths and conventions?

As I have stated earlier, the value of these Afro-American critical studies lies in the fact that they identify Afro-American cultural patterns and forms, or choose certain Afro-American world
views, to produce Afro-American literary traditions, canons, and
myths. They establish a critical matrix that receives Afro-
American texts more favorably, that defines the worth of Afro-
American literature within an Afro-American cultural context.
But what these Afro-American critical studies fail to take into
consideration is that Afro-American myths, definitions, and linguistic structures are not "natural" in their use by Afro-
American writers or by the dominant American literary establishment. They are produced. Further, any use of them in
ignorance of the nature of their production or function can lead
to an entrapment. Afro-American myths and conventions are inextricably tied to the production of Afro-American texts that in
turn determines which images or representations of the Afro-
American will appear before the American public. To fail to examine this process is to be entrapped into believing that these
images and representations are reflections of the Afro-American
social reality rather than productions of it—productions that

have political and social functions, be they Afro-American or American.

With an awareness of the role literary production plays in the definition of Afro-American literature, we can begin to see how literature is one of the social institutions within the cultural apparatus, or even within oppressed, marginal social groups within society. We can see how literature provides indices and coherent myths for social subjects (individuals) as they seek equilibrium. But when a racial or cultural group is not in control of its literary productions and when a racial or cultural group fails to discern clearly the different world views within the race or culture that inform the production of the literature, as in the case of Afro-America, it must become aware of the ideological and literary forces that produce literature. It must also be concerned with whose interest literary productions serve. Thus far, most Afro-American critical practices are silent on literary production.

The following chapters will examine Afro-American texts and the images and representations of the Afro-American they present in light of literary production and the role of the power-conflict that marks the discursive context today. They will trace this power-conflict from the nineteenth century to the present. They will examine the American social movement of the 1960s, its effects on the production of Afro-American texts, and its challenge to the constraints of the dominant literary discourse. Second, these chapters will work from the assumption that literature is not a "natural" category with inherent qualities by which all literary texts can be judged. Instead, they will assume that literature is a social institution that functions to reproduce certain discursive literary assumptions. They will examine how in reproducing these assumptions it excludes, by the mere nature of its formation, other literary texts. Last, these chapters will focus on how literary discourses are permeated with power and thereby can appropriate, exclude, or subordinate any text that enters their discursive formations.

Chapter 2. The Dominant American Literary Establishment and the Production of the Afro-American Text

This chapter deals with the dominant American ideological apparatus (dominant society) and its relations to Afro-American texts. It examines how the ruling literary establishment, a set of literary practices and institutions, affected the production of Afro-American texts and Afro-American images prior to the social movements of the 1960s. The succeeding chapter will examine what happened to this relationship among the literary establishment, its literary practices and institutions, and the production of Afro-American texts and images when social movements of the sixties attempted to delegitimate the dominant American society.

James Baldwin, in a poignant interview with Studs Turkel, argues that in America the Afro-American represents a difference, an Other—a level of human experience that the dominant society denies: "To be a Negro in this country . . . is never to be looked at. What white people see when they do look at you is what they have invested you with. And what they have invested you with is all the agony, pain, anger, and passion and torment, sin, death, and hell in which everyone in this country is terrified. You [the Negro] represent a level of experience which Americans deny."[1] The Afro-American is a descendant of the slaves, while the white American is a descendant of the master. The Afro-American comes from Africa; the white American comes from Europe. Slavery and later racial segregation produced for the

Afro-American a condition that includes suffering and pain; the white American belongs to a culture that views pain and suffering as aberrants.

To the white American, the Afro-American is the Other—that which introduces the gaps, incompleteness, and contradictions in the definition or constitution of the subject or object. The nature of the interaction between the two reflects this difference. When the bourgeois, rational individual is confronted by the Other, argues Roland Barthes, he "blinds himself, ignores and denies him [the Other], or else transforms him into himself." When the individual cannot assimilate the Other, the "Other becomes a pure object, a spectacle, a clown. Relegated to the confines of humanity, he no longer threatens the security of the home."[2] Since the presence of the Afro-American as a different type of ontological structure allows whites to pass a judgment on themselves that they would rather deny, it is excluded. Whites either invest the Afro-American with myths and images that integrate him into the "natural order of things," thereby negating his differences; categorize him as exotica or a spectacle which isolates and neutralizes him as the Other; or ignore his existence completely. The exclusion of the Afro-American has more to do with the discursive formation that defines whites' definition of reality than it has to do with intentional, motivated racism. But the images and myths invested in the Afro-American become integral practices within the dominant ideological apparatus. They become a part of the myth of an American consensus—its process of normalization, its principle of unity and cohesion. They provide the ruling social order with an explanation to overcome the contradiction the Afro-American represents within its discursive formation. The ideological apparatus reproduces itself in its various practices by reproducing these Afro-American myths and images as Other. "The pervasive cultural nationalism of the West," argues Sylvia Wynter, "invites as its negation an inversion of its own presuppositions. The past has been reinvented as ideology by the West, to sustain the West's consciousness of itself as subject, a consciousness which needed the negation of the Other, the non-West."[3]

To show specifically how literary practices and institutions within the ruling literary establishment produce Afro-American texts and determine which images of the Afro-American will appear in them, let us examine how these practices and institutions responded to two particular Afro-American texts: Zora Neale Hurston's *Their Eyes Were Watching God* (1937) and Richard Wright's *Native Son* (1940). Then let us examine their response to the production of Afro-American texts from the late nineteenth century to the 1960s.

Hurston's *Their Eyes Were Watching God* concerns the romantic quest of Janie Starks, a black woman who has the fortitude and intuitive wisdom to transcend the dehumanizing definitions —manifested in her grandmother and in the men she marries— of a rational bourgeois society, and to find her inner voice, her identity. Here Hurston turns upside down many of the myths and stereotypes about the Afro-American. Rejecting the usual pathological portrayal of blacks, she exhumes spiritual, emotional, and other aspects of Afro-American consciousness—captured in folklore and folk wisdom—that had been excluded. Hurston is trying to approach a definition of existence where the resolution to the text's problems are reached differently by straining the ability of generic techniques to effect a closure within the text's discursive formation. To effect its closure, the novel formulates a counter or inverted worldview—manifested in Janie's first two husbands and her grandmother—that is trapped in mainstream bourgeois contexts, values, and codes. But the novel also and ultimately presents a character, Janie, who enables us to see the constraints of established ideological stereotypes and abstract constructs. Through Janie the text produces an experience whose lived and theoretical concept of history is *different* from the one the dominant American society imposes.

When *Their Eyes Were Watching God* was published, it was received distantly and unenthusiastically. The *New York Times Book Review* describes it "as her [Hurston's] third novel again about her own people—and it is beautiful."[4] The *Saturday Review of Literature* writes that "you will have no difficulty believing in the Negro community which Zora Neale Hurston has either reconstructed or imagined in this novel."[5] The reviewer, George Stevens, goes on to say: "The town of Eatonville is as

real in these pages as Jacksonville is in the pages of Rand
McNally."[6] When *Time* magazine reviewed Hurston's novel
along with Walter Turpin's *These Low Grounds,* the reviewer
wrote of both books as sociological tracts: "Both Negro author
Turpin and Negro author Hurston paint their racial pictures
with little shading in glistening blacks and lurid tans."[7]

But besides describing Hurston's conception "of these simple
Florida Negroes," a description that has a shade of the exotic, as
"unaffected and really beautiful," the reviewers and critics of
this novel saw no "universal" or lasting qualities. The novel was
not the kind of writing they defined as "great" literature. Even
certain major Afro-American reviewers categorized Hurston's
novel as exotica. In his review, Richard Wright argued that
"Miss Hurston seems to have no desire whatever to move in the
direction of serious fiction. . . . The sensory sweep of her novel
carries no theme, no message, no thought. In the main, her novel
is not addressed to the Negro, but to a white audience whose
chauvinistic tastes she knows how to satisfy." He saw Hurston's
art as a "minstrel technique."[8] In this unfavorable review, the
reader witnesses Wright accepting uncritically a definition of literature that excludes Hurston's novel as "serious fiction."

Since Hurston's novel was not received favorably by writers
and critics, it went out of print—except for small printings in
Fawcett paperback in 1965 and by Greenwood Press in 1969
and limited editions on Negro Universities Press—until 1981
when the University of Illinois Press brought it back out in
paperback.

Why did a novel that tells a romantic story remain mostly out
of print from 1937 to 1981? Why did a novel that chronicles
successfully a heroic attempt to find inner peace, identity, and
one's own voice remain mostly out of print from 1937 to 1981?
Was it because Hurston was black? Richard Wright's *Native Son,*
published in 1940, was selected for the Book-of-the-Month Club.
Native Son never went out of print. Did Hurston's novel go out
of print because she was a woman? Gwendolyn Brooks and
Margaret Walker were two of the major poets published and revered in the 1940s and 1950s. Margaret Walker published widely
in American poetry journals through the 1930s and 1940s—

Crisis (1934), *Poetry* (1937, 1938, 1939), *New Challenge* (1937), *Creative Writing* (1938), and *Virginia Quarterly* (1955). Her most noted collection of poems, *For My People,* published in 1942 by Yale University Press, won the Yale Award for Younger Poets. This noted collection went through seven printings and did not go out of print until the middle of the 1970s. Walker's *October's Journey* was published in 1970 by Broadside Press, an independent black publishing house.

Gwendolyn Brooks, another black woman poet, received similar literary acclaim. In addition to publishing poems in noted mainstream literary journals, Brooks was published by Harper and Row, one of America's major publishing houses, from 1945 to 1968 when she decided to leave Harper and Row for Broadside Press. Her books of poems remained in print throughout, and the publication of *Annie Allen* in 1949 was instrumental in her being awarded the Pulitzer Prize for poetry in 1950 and being designated the poet laureate of Illinois.

Walker and Brooks were published and revered in the 1940s and 1950s because they used certain poetic stanzas that were considered standard by established literary practices. Robert E. Moss, in an article entitled "The Arts of Black America," writes that the elder statesmen among black poets—notably Robert Hayden, Melvin B. Tolson, Margaret Walker, and early Gwendolyn Brooks—achieved recognition from the literary establishment because they adjusted "their timbre and rhythm, their style and vocabulary, to the requirements of mainstream verse, although their subject matter was sometimes racial."[9] Walker's and Brook's move from the mainstream publishing houses to Broadside Press in the late sixties and early seventies, along with their writing a freer verse form, signaled the emergence of the black arts movement and the freedom for Afro-American writers to write for a black audience.

Ann Petry's *The Street* (1946) is another novel by a black woman that was acclaimed widely during this period. It became a national bestseller that commanded immediate attention. *The Street* tells the story of a young black woman, Lutie Johnson, who, having lost her husband during the Depression, tries to make a decent life for herself and her son in Harlem. The novel chronicles the degradation, symbolized by her apartment and the environment of the streets, she must endure. It also shows the effects of this degraded existence on Lutie's life. The novel met with enthusiastic reviews and was awarded the Houghton Mifflin Fellowship Prize. Reviewing *The Street* in *Phylon,* Alain Locke wrote, "The artistic success of the year is, of course, Ann Petry's *The Street.*"[10] Arna Bontemps wrote in the *New York Herald Tribune Weekly Book Review,* "As a novelist Petry is an un-blushing realist. Her recreation of the street has left out none of its essential character."[11] In *Common Ground* Henry Tracy claimed, "*The Street* is an outstanding novel from any angle,"[12] and Alfred Butterfield echoed these sentiments in the *New York Times Book Review:* "*The Street* is a work of close documentation and intimate perception."[13]

This brings us back to our original question: why did Hurston's *Their Eyes Were Watching God* go out of print in 1937 and remain mostly out of print until 1981? Can we say that Wright, Walker, Brooks, and Petry were simply better writers than Hurston? If so how do we deal with the enormous attention that Hurston and *Their Eyes Were Watching God* are receiving in the 1980s? The novel has been resurrected and is now taught in feminist courses, Afro-American literature courses, and some general American literature courses. Hurston's other books *—Dust Tracks on a Road, Mules and Men, Jonah's Gourd Vine* —are back in print and there are several recent critical studies of Hurston's works by Mary Helen Washington, Alice Walker, Sherley Ann Williams, and Darwin Turner. Robert Hemenway recently published a biography of Hurston, and Alice Walker has just edited a *Zora Neale Hurston Reader.*

Perhaps, we can best answer the question if we shift our investigation from race and sex exclusively to an examination of definitions, assumptions, and criteria used to determine the worth of literary texts during the 1930s and 1940s. The neglect of Hurston's novel can be best explained first by acknowledging the literary presence of the naturalist movement in American literature during the first half of the twentieth century; second, by identifying naturalism's criteria, standards, and assumptions about literature—its model for determining the worth of literary texts; and third, by examining how closely Hurston, as compared to Wright and Petry, meets those naturalist standards and criteria.

The literary texts of Frank Norris and Stephen Crane, published in the 1890s, began a naturalist movement in American letters which reached its peak with the publication of Theodore Dreiser's *An American Tragedy* in 1925, and manifested itself during the 1940s and 1950s in the works of Afro-American writers such as Richard Wright, Ann Petry, Chester Himes, William Attaway, and Willard Motley. During the first half of the twentieth century, the naturalist movement was one mode of writing that dominated the American literary scene. It became a kind of literature that was judged "fine." Naturalism's literary themes and motifs—determinism, survival, violence, and taboo— became the standards by which the worth of a literary text was assessed and judged. These themes were a part of the definitions of reality that belonged to the ruling ideological apparatus. They were tied to naturalism's ontological structures; and the resolutions of these themes in literary expression function as indices for realism within this ideological apparatus.

Therefore, when Wright's *Native Son* was published in 1940, it was reviewed, assessed, and judged according to how effectively it expressed these naturalist themes and motifs. Malcolm Cowley, the reviewer for the *New Republic,* placed *Native Son* in the company of other "great" naturalist texts: "*Native Son* is the most impressive American novel I have read since *The Grapes of Wrath.*"[14] The *New York Times Book Review* opened its discussion of *Native Son* by pointing out its similarities to the naturalist themes of Dreiser's *An American Tragedy:*

> A ready way to show the importance of this novel is to call it the Negro "American Tragedy" and to compare it roughly with Dreiser's masterpiece. Both deal seriously and powerfully with the problem of social maladjustment, with environment and individual behavior, and subsequently with crime and punishment. Both are tragedies and Dreiser's white boy and Wright's black boy are equally killed in the electric chair not for being criminals—since the crime in each case was unpremeditated—but for being social misfits. The pattern in

both books is similar: the family, the adolescent, the lure of money and sex, fortuitous events, murder, trial and death. The conclusion in both is that society is to blame, that the environment into which each was born forced upon them their crimes, that they were the particular victims of a general injustice.[15]

The *Nation*'s review of *Native Son* begins:

For terror in narrative, utter and compelling, there are few pages in modern American literature which will compare with this story of the few little days which carried Bigger Thomas, Negro from Mississippi to Chicago, from bullying cowardice through murder to the position of black fiend against the hating world, hunted across rooftops in the snow. It is authentic, powerful writing. . . . I doubt that Bigger Thomas proves any more about the Negro than he does about the world. Man's inhumanity to man did not begin in Mississippi. It did not end with Bigger Thomas in Chicago. What Mr. Wright has written again and wonderfully . . . is the very ancient story of all criminals who have advanced through the cruel caprices of environment into the frenzy of unequal enmity against a continually imperfect world.[16]

For these reviewers, Richard Wright in *Native Son* did not, like Hurston in *Their Eyes Were Watching God,* paint "racial pictures" or capture the "really beautiful . . . simple Florida Negroes." Instead, he wrote the "very ancient story" of "man's inhumanity to man." According to these reviewers, Wright was writing about certain themes—social maladjustment, the individual and his environment, criminals, murder, violence, and death—that dominant critical practices, at least at this period in American literary history, defined as more worthy and "universal" than the quest for identity, personal freedom, and happiness.

In addition, the image of the Afro-American projected in *Native Son* is one of pathological victimization, while the image of the Afro-American in *Their Eyes Were Watching God* is one of independent assertiveness and free will. Naturalism carries with it an image of man as a victim. The determinism of naturalism makes it very easy to think that the victim is "natural," an inevitable response to the "way things are."

Thus it was Wright's ability to produce a cultural object whose effect and function generated a popular American literary taste, or the meaning of a particular accepted literary experience, that made *Native Son* a national bestseller. Critics and reviewers sent signals to awarding agencies that *Native Son* was a "great" novel. *Native Son* was selected for the Book-of-the-Month-Club. This certification caused *Native Son* to remain in print, while Hurston's failure or refusal to meet an established literary taste caused *Their Eyes Were Watching God* to go out of print in 1937. Only with the rise of the feminist movement and the black nationalist movement in the 1960s and 1970s, with their different aesthetic standards and literary tastes, was *Their Eyes Were Watching God* placed in a new constellation where its worth and value were reassessed and redefined.

In examining the favorable reception during the 1940s of Wright's *Native Son* and Petry's *The Street* and the unfavorable reception of Hurston's novel, the reader can see how normative criticism functions: as an active and ongoing part of literary tastes and theories of literature. Since a literary text has no meaning except that which is imputed by criticism, normative criticism establishes a "universal" model, albeit ideological, that corrects literary texts. The worth and value of literary texts are determined by how closely they approximate the model. *Native Son* and *The Street* approximated ruling ideological models more closely than *Their Eyes Were Watching God.*

All Afro-American writers have had to contend with the dominant American ideological cultural apparatus and its literary practices and institutions, which, by the mere nature of their systems of formation, exclude certain Afro-American texts and images. Although there is no evidence that the motives and strategies of these practices are consciously racist, their effects can be interpreted as racist. Afro-American writers have either accepted and reproduced established American images of the Afro-American, or they have moved to counter these images. The publication, review, distribution, and reception of their texts are tied inextricably to the kinds of images, values, defined literary experiences, and stereotypes they reproduce.

In the late nineteenth century Charles Chesnutt, considered

the first Afro-American novelist of any national literary reputation, wrote of how publishing houses censored his attempts to write about certain sensitive aspects of Afro-American life. In a letter to George Washington Cable (5 June 1890), Chesnutt laments: "The kind of stuff I could write, if I were not all the time oppressed by the fear that this line or this sentiment would offend somebody's prejudices, jar on somebody's American-trained sense of propriety."[17] But Chesnutt did dare to write about unsanctioned aspects of Afro-American life. Before Chesnutt published the short story, "The Goophered Grapevine," which draws upon Afro-American folklore, America's image of the Afro-American in Afro-American folklore—except for William Wells Brown's *My Southern Home* (1880) which was out of print—had been drawn from the stories Joel Chandler Harris collected and published in the 1880s. These stories, as Darwin Turner points out, are "amusing, genteel, moralistic children's tales narrated most frequently by Uncle Remus, a kindly slave who, despite occasional petulance with his mistress, seems pleased to serve his white master—old and young."[18] Harris employed this passive and docile image of the Afro-American in his novels during most of the 1880s. This image complemented the image of the happy slave that Thomas Nelson Page and others needed to create the myth that the Afro-American had been a happy slave in the ideal society of the Southern plantation.[19]

The reiteration in the works of Harris, Page, and others of the image of the Afro-American as a docile, passive, nonthreatening victim becomes a constant in the literature of white Americans during the latter half of the nineteenth century. Even Mark Twain's *Huckleberry Finn,* which gives a sensitive and humane portrayal of the slave Jim, reinforces this image. In escaping society and his father, Huck Finn finds himself alone on an island with Miss Watson's slave Jim, where he comes to know Jim in ways that normative society's practices preclude. For Huck, Jim becomes a person with all the complexities and impulses of any other human being. As a result he can no longer view Jim as just a "nigger" who is subhuman and therefore deserving of his subhuman status. This new perception of Jim creates a crisis in

Huck's conscience that forces him to question some societal definitions and assumptions.

But in producing this portrayal of Huck, the text produces a safe, passive, and docile image of Jim. Within the text's discursive formation, Jim has no inclination to rebel against slavery, to take control over his destiny. In ignoring Jim's Otherness, Twain reproduces a dominant American literary convention or practice that presents a safe, docile, nonthreatening image of the Afro-American as a "natural" in the order of things.

Uncle Tom, the black slave in Harriet Beecher Stowe's *Uncle Tom's Cabin,* also reiterates the macrosign of the safe docile darky who trusts and seems pleased to serve his white master. When hard times fall on the house of Shelby, Uncle Tom, who had been promised his freedom, becomes the payment for the debts. He is torn from his wife, home, and children and consigned to the terror-ridden slave markets of the lower Mississippi. With numerous chances to escape, Uncle Tom remains loyal to his master.

Reacting to this image of the Afro-American produced by Harris, Page, Stowe, and others, Chesnutt wrote to Cable: "Thomas Nelson Page and Harry S. Edwards depict the sentimental and devoted Negro, who prefers kicks to half pence. . . . I notice that all of the many Negroes . . . whose virtues have been given to the world in the magazine press recently have been blacks, full blooded, and their chief virtues have been their dog-like fidelity to their old masters, for whom they have been willing to sacrifice almost life itself."[20] Chesnutt, like many of his successors for the next hundred years, set out to refute and repudiate this dehumanizing, safe image of the Afro-American. In *The Conjure Woman* (1899) Chesnutt presents Uncle Julius McAdoo, a shrewd freedman of mixed blood who uses witchcraft to manipulate white people. In *The House Behind the Cedars* (1900), he explores the problems confronting the interracial Afro-American. Chesnutt had difficulty getting both novels published.

In *The Marrow of Tradition* (1901), Chesnutt recounts the massacre of blacks during the 1898 election in Wilmington, North Carolina, where blacks were disfranchised. Through the characters of Dr. William Miller and Josh Green, *The Marrow of*

Tradition produces images of the Afro-American that counter those of Page, Harris, Twain, Stowe, and others. Dr. Miller is a rational intellectual who has a dedicated, realistic approach to the injustices within society. Josh Green, whose father was murdered by the Klu Klux Klan and whose mother retreated into idiocy, is the black rebel who dedicates his life to hatred and vengeance. Frustrated by the reception of *The Marrow of Tradition,* Chesnutt wrote, "I suppose I shall have to drop the attempt at realism, and try to make them like other folks. . . . I shall write as every man must do, to please editors, to please the public."[21] But Chesnutt never made this concession; instead, he ceased writing. He had failed, admittedly, to convince America that the Afro-American was more than the myths and stereotypes projected by Harris and Page. Chesnutt was writing about the Otherness in Afro-American life that dominant American literary practices—editors, review journals and magazines, and publishers—would rather ignore or deny. Consequently the sales of his books, which soon went out of print, never equaled his expectations. In 1928, upon receiving the NAACP's Spingarn Medal, Chesnutt explained the sudden halt to his literary career in 1905: "My books were written, from one point of view, a generation too soon. There was no such demand then as there is now for books by and about colored people. And I was writing against the trend of public opinion on the race question at that particular time. And I had to sell my books chiefly to white readers."[22]

Other Afro-American writers of Chesnutt's generation and earlier either catered to established literary myths, images, and stereotypes, or were excluded from literary success. William Wells Brown's *Clotel; or The President's Daughter* (1853), which deals with the affair of a U.S. president and his black concubine, was published in London. The American edition underwent extensive revision—deleting many of those nonconformist themes that would, to use Chesnutt's words, "offend somebody's prejudices, jar somebody's American-trained sense of propriety." Brown's novel remained out of print until the upsurge of Afro-American literature in the 1960s. Harriet Wilson's *Our Nig, or Sketches from the Life of a Free Black,* published in 1859 and addressed to her black brethren rather than to the Northern white liberals, deals with the destitution, due to racism, of the "free" black in the North. *Our Nig* subsequently was lost from collective American and Afro-American literary traditions and was not brought back into print until 1983 by Vintage. Similarly, in *Contending Forces* (1899), Pauline Hopkins, like Stowe in *Uncle Tom's Cabin,* writes of injustices suffered by blacks at the hands of whites. But Hopkins, unlike Stowe, deals with certain nonconformist themes—the rape of black women by white men, blacks helping themselves rather than being "natural" victims dependent on benevolent whites. The novel went out of print immediately and was not reissued until 1978. Stowe's novel remained in print throughout and is considered a major American novel of the nineteenth century. Likewise Martin Delany's *Blake, or The Huts of America,* written in 1861, deals with blacks asserting themselves against exclusionary American practices that pose a menace to their livelihood, and was not published in novel form until 1970.

In a final example, Paul Laurence Dunbar, a contemporary of Charles Chesnutt, was also affected by which literary images of the Afro-American he could present and still find a publisher. In *The Fanatics* (1901), Dunbar reproduces the safe, docile darky image of the Afro-American. Set during the Civil War, *The Fanatics* examines the actions and thoughts of two white families: one sympathetic to the Union and the other to the Confederacy. As the two families act out their dramas on center stage, the novel (which cannot deal with the Civil War without dealing with blacks) eschews images of rebellious, assertive blacks and presents Nigger Ed who, as Addison Gayle points out, is "loyal, obedient, and subservient, and who has 'a picturesque knack for lying.' "[23] Only in *The Sports of the Gods* (1902) does Dunbar transcend established myths and stereotypes. But in this transcendence, he actually moves the image of the Afro-American into a sensational, naturalistic trend or literary practice that has dominated American literary tastes since Crane and Norris. Addison Gayle attributes the adoption of naturalism and its sensational portrayal of blacks to the fact that Dunbar wrote exclusively for white audiences. In order for whites to buy his books he had to reproduce expected literary conventions and practices.

Thus, during the last half of the nineteenth century and the early years of the twentieth century, dominant American literary practices produced particular kinds of Afro-American images and texts. Their discursive formations praised certain Afro-American texts—articulating their formal adherence to normative criteria and pointing out their contribution to a discursive knowledge. Those Afro-American texts that dealt with nonconformist themes and subjects—aggressive, dignified, intelligent, or assertive blacks—were ignored. They were either aborted at the editor's desk, published in Europe, or never published at all.

But even Afro-American texts—such as Dunbar's *The Sports of the Gods* and *The Fanatics*—that were sanctioned by editors, publishers, and critics were considered as *Other* and were not awarded the privilege of entering the canon of American literature. This established literary practice of permitting and excluding certain Afro-American texts and not legitimating any, as the remainder of this chapter will point out, affected the production of Afro-American texts until the 1960s.

Just as Afro-American writers in the late nineteenth century had to struggle with the constraints of the ruling literary practices, in the 1920s and 1930s Afro-American writers contended with similar constraints. In America during the 1920s a new but equally repressive image of the Afro-American became popular, as white intellectuals began to respond not only to the disorder and chaos brought on by World War I but also to the human consequences of mass, modern, industrial society. Many of these intellectuals used Freudian psychology to interpret their predicament rationally and intellectually. According to Freud, the human animal is prevented by civilization's social forces from attaining fulfillment. If intellectual, rational man could strip away civilizing artifices, he could be more immediate, more passionate, more healthy. He could love, dance, and live with freedom and abandon.[24]

After World War I it became a more salient belief among white intellectuals that they were enslaved by dehumanizing, puritanical moral codes and practices that made them emotional cripples. They came to view Afro-American life as their salvation; they saw it as immediate, instinctive, and honest, and be-

lieved that all aspects of the Afro-American's life—his music, his
dance, his art—uncoiled deep inner tensions.[25] For these intellectuals Afro-American culture offered relief from the relentless
engine of industrial America. It functioned as a ghost for these
white intellectuals' primal nature and it reminded them of the
"essential" self they felt they had lost on the way to civility.

Carl Van Vechten, a collector of rare objects and rare people,
was one of the many white intellectuals who became associated
culturally with blacks in Harlem in the 1920s. In *Nigger Heaven* he
portrays Afro-American life as exotic and primitive. Harlem is not
portrayed as monolithic, for he shows each stratum of the black
community—the black upper class, the black middle class, and the
"natural" black class. The normative figure is Scarlet Creeper, who
is dapperly attired at all times and who is knowledgeable in the
ways of Harlem life—sweet men, pimps, gamblers, and prostitutes.
As his name implies, Creeper is free, easygoing, and colorful. Characters like Mary Love, who are in disharmony with this Harlem
environment, are considered tragic.

Van Vechten's novel remained for months on the bestseller
list. It was the culmination of a general effort by white writers in
the 1920s to make the Afro-American primal state an artistic
subject. *Nigger Heaven* (1926) was preceded by Gertrude Stein's
Three Lives (1909), Eugene O'Neill's *Emperor Jones* (1920) and
All God's Chillun Got Wings (1924), E. E. Cummings's *The
Enormous Room* (1922), Waldo Frank's *Holiday* (1923),
Sherwood Anderson's *Dark Laughter* (1925), and Du Bois
Heyward's *Porgy* (1925). *Nigger Heaven* was followed by Julia
Peterkin's *Scarlet Sister Mary* (1928), which was awarded the
Pulitzer Prize. All of these texts reproduced the image of the Af-
ro-American as exotic and "naturally" primitive.

During the 1920s, if Afro-American writers were to publish
and sell, they had to reproduce this particular image of the Afro-
American, or derivatives of it. In 1923 American writers received Jean Toomer's *Cane* enthusiastically. In a letter to
Toomer, Sherwood Anderson wrote, "Your work [Cane] is of a
special significance to me because it is the first negro work I
have seen that strikes me as being really negro. . . . You are the
only negro . . . who seems really to have consciously the artist's

impulse."[26] In his foreword to *Cane,* Waldo Frank said, "A poet has arisen among our American youth who has known how to turn the essences of materials of his Southland into the essences and materials of literature."[27] Allen Tate wrote Toomer to praise his "genuine and innovative quality of technique."[28] What attracted these men of American letters to *Cane* was Toomer's ability to reproduce certain acceptable literary practices of the period, such as the experimental form and the primitive image of the Afro-American. *Cane,* a collage of sketches, songs, and poetry about Afro-American life, portrays Southern blacks as instinctive, immediate, sexually free, happy in misery, and close to nature and the Southern soil. It presents black life as existing in humanity's primal state. Characters such as Fern, Becky, Carma, Esther, Louisa, and Karintha are presented without consciousness, as human beings who live by their instincts. They embody unconsciously all the joy and pain, terrors and fears associated with the land.

But Toomer's representation of black life in *Cane* is silent on chivalrous gentlemen, the fair decaying mansions, mammies, cotton, and pickaninnies. It is also silent on the hate, the rebellious young blacks. For Anderson, O'Neill, Van Vechten, and others, *Cane,* to use the words of Waldo Frank, "is the South" because it reproduces a dominant literary experience or myth.

Although Toomer's *Cane* uses established literary conventions and stereotypes—naturalism to interpret black urban life—it uses an experimental form and aspects of Eastern philosophy called Oupensky, to attempt a solution outside these practices to the Afro-American dilemma. Underneath these established literary practices and conventions, Toomer reveals the black man's internalization of racial conflicts, his retreat to the South, his rejection of the philosophy of the black bourgeoisie, and his rejection of the past and eventual marginality of all ideologies. Using an experimental form and Eastern philosophy, Toomer grapples with his materials to map out a new way for blacks to seek identity. We see Toomer strain the ability of generic techniques to effect a closure within the discursive formations of accepted literary practices, to signify an experience whose lived and theoretical concept of reality is different from those produced by mainstream literary practices. Toomer's failure to reach a resolution in *Cane* indicates his rebellion against normative literary conventions and stereotypes. But although the text works against these stereotypes, its reproduction of them allows reviewers and critics to appropriate it.

After this initial attention in the 1920s, Toomer's *Cane* vanished from the memories of these literary men. Darwin Turner writes:

> In 1923, twenty-eight-year-old Jean Toomer . . . was one of the brightest stars in this galaxy. . . . Twenty-five years later . . . Toomer was not being discussed or studied. I was almost embarrassed to confess my admiration for Toomer's work because surely . . . if the man is as brilliant as I believe him to be, some of my professors of American literature would require me to read his work, or at least they would mention his name occasionally.[29]

In 1928 two other texts were published by Afro-Americans—Rudolph Fisher's *Walls of Jericho* and Claude McKay's *Home to Harlem*—that reproduced the "primitive" image of the Afro-American. Although like *Cane* these texts were, in Nathan Huggins's words, "something more than merely cynical efforts to exploit white fancy," both reproduced themes suggested by Van Vechten and both met commercial success.[30] McKay's *Home to Harlem,* the first Afro-American novel placed on the bestseller list, ostensibly chronicles Jake's search for Felice, a prostitute who serviced him once on a trip home. But at a more profound and intellectual level, the novel concerns Jake's search for a primal home, first recognized in Felice, that exists outside the context of rational, bourgeois Western civilization. In pandering to white vogue in black primitivism, *Home to Harlem* reproduced the literary images and conventions necessary to be appropriated. And any genuine literary interests McKay and other Harlem Renaissance writers had, outside those defined by the ideological cultural apparatus, were excluded or ignored.

These reproductions of and exclusions of certain themes, images, and subjects were reinforced by the patronage system. Most Afro-American writers of this period had white patrons who

paid them stipends to write. In his early years in the United
States McKay was supported financially by Frank Harris of
Pearson's Magazine. Later in his literary career he was supported
by Max Eastman of *Liberator* and the Catholic church. Zora
Neale Hurston, Louise Thompson, and Langston Hughes were
supported by the same elderly Park Avenue matron. All three recall her the same way—beautiful, generous, with a strong pen-
chant for "primitive" tastes. Linking her "primitive" tastes to
the Afro-American, Hughes writes: "Concerning Negroes, she felt
that they were America's great link with the primitive, and that
they had something very precious to give to the Western World.
She felt that there was mystery and mysticism and spontaneous
harmony in their souls, but that many of them had let the white
world pollute and contaminate that mystery and harmony, and
make of it something cheap and ugly."[31] The patrons did not
support these writers and just let them write. Instead, they expected these writers to cater to their tasks for the "primitive."
When Hughes wrote "Advertisement for the Waldorf-Astoria," a
poem about the cold, hunger, and despair he saw "on the way to
my friend's home on Park Avenue," his patron responded, "It's
not you. . . . It's a powerful poem! But it's not you."[32]

Further, these patrons enjoyed black writers for their own
"primitive" qualities, as Max Eastman makes clear in describing
his attraction to McKay: "His laughter at the frailties of his
friends and enemies, no matter which—that high, half-wailing
falsetto laugh of the recklessly delighted Darky—was the center
of my joy in him throughout our friendship of more than thirty
years."[33] Langston Hughes, Wallace Thurman, and Louise
Thompson describe how Zora Neale Hurston staged the "primitive," pagan black image for her white patron. Hughes writes:

> Of this "niggeratti," Zora Neale Hurston was certainly the
> most amusing. Only to reach a wider audience, need she ever
> write books—because she is a perfect book of entertainment in
> herself. In her youth she was always getting scholarships and
> things from wealthy white people, some of whom simply paid
> her just to sit around and represent the Negro race for them,
> she did it in such a racy fashion. . . . To many of her white

friends, no doubt, she was a perfect "darkie," in the nice meaning they give the term—that is a naive, childlike, sweet humorous, and highly colored Negro.[34]

But many of these Harlem Renaissance writers were determined to strain or violate existing literary conventions to produce different images and stereotypes. In incorporating Afro-American language and folklore in his poetry, Langston Hughes wrote about an Afro-American who was different from the one produced by traditional literary practices and conventions. He wanted to get at the essence of a different Afro-American: "I was only an American Negro—who had lived the surface of Africa and the rhythms of Africa—but I was not Africa. I was Chicago and Kansas City and Broadway and Harlem."[35] The Jessie B. Simples in Hughes's short stories and other characters in his poetry are not "darkies" but American Negroes—a synthesis of Africa and America, of rational and nonrational. But the language of the dominant American ideological apparatus by definition does not have the vocabulary or the classification for the Other that Hughes hoped to present. Consequently that apparatus places him in the exotic category where his aims and intentions are redefined and appropriated.

In the 1940s and 1950s, as I stated earlier, literary naturalism for the most part determined what images of the Afro-American were produced. But there were other existential Afro-American texts—Gwendolyn Brooks's *Maud Martha* (1953), William Demby's *Beetlecreek* (1950), and Ellison's *Invisible Man* (1952) in particular—that did not portray the Afro-American as a pathological, violent victim who was, to use the words of Zora Neale Hurston, "tragically colored." These texts, especially *Maud Martha* and *Beetlecreek,* were excluded or ignored by the dominant naturalist literary practice. However, they were received by other reviewers and critics within the literary establishment. Brooks's *Maud Martha,* in a collage of sketches and love scenes, traces the life of a dark-skinned girl from childhood to the time she has her first child. In the slums of Chicago, this character's life is simple and ordinary: childhood, school, deaths of relatives, dates with young men, envy of sister's beauty, and at last marriage. In these loosely assembled incidents that pile up to have a single effect on the reader, the text produces an Afro-American social reality where poverty and racism exist. But, most important, what emerges in the text is a heroine who functions to turn unhappiness and anger into a joke, to show human sensitivity and warmth in the midst of poverty and racism. There are no murders and there is no violence. In *Maud Martha,* life in its vitality becomes larger than poverty and racism.

Although it was received warmly by some mainstream reviewers, *Maud Martha* was ignored by Afro-American naturalists and by major critical studies of the Afro-American novel. Robert Hemenway's *The Black Novelist,* Addison Gayle's *The Way of the New World,* Phyllis Klotman's *Another Man Gone,* Houston A. Baker's *Singers of Daybreak,* George Kent's *Blackness and the Adventure of Western Culture,* and M. G. Cooke's *Modern Black Novelists* have all ignored *Maud Martha.* Brooks was obviously not writing a kind of literature they defined as "good." Only with the feminist movement of the 1970s was *Maud Martha* exhumed from the archives.

William Demby's *Beetlecreek* was also ignored by Afro-American naturalists but was praised by others. It was ignored in all of the aforementioned major studies except Gayle's *The Way of the New World.* The novel is the story of a black youth, Johnny, who arrives from Pittsburgh to live with his aunt and uncle in Beetlecreek, a rural Southern town. Johnny wants desperately to be accepted by the other youths in the community, but he is frightened, repelled, and attracted by their crude sexual practices. Finding himself alone, Johnny befriends Bill Trapp, a white man who lives in the midst of this black community and who is also a recluse. The relationship between Johnny and Bill Trapp, both outsiders searching for identities, is repudiated by the black community which cannot see beyond its ideological and racial constructs. Johnny ends up killing Bill Trapp.

Beetlecreek moves beyond certain racial stereotypes and abstract constructs that were at the core of the protest novel, to deal with alienation and the search for identity that resulted from the limitations and constraints of these racial constructs and stereotypes. It uses certain existential literary concepts—

such as alienation, the search—to effect a closure within existing generic techniques.

Beetlecreek was reviewed favorably by mainstream and white American reviewers. In his review in the *Nation,* Ernest Jones wrote: "Unlike Langston Hughes and Richard Wright and William Gardner Smith, Mr. Demby has avoided the inevitable pitfalls which beset the American Negro who writes out of his own experience. His book is only in a secondary sense about 'The Negro Problem.' "[36] In his afterword in the 1965 Avon edition, Robert Hill argued: "*Beetlecreek* belongs to that tradition of literature that questions the human condition, that is concerned with the interior meaning and reality of man's fate . . . Demby does not protest against the universal human condition for, as he tells us in a later work, 'life is existence and existence is sacred.' " In his introduction to Demby's *The Catacombs,* Robert Bone commented: "*Beetlecreek* . . . is a young man's novel: rebellious, but thoroughly controlled in execution. The point of view is existentialist, the tone expatriate. The style . . . reveals a man in desperate retreat from the smug parochialism of mid-century America." But despite this attention from noted critics such as Bone and Hill, *Beetlecreek* soon passed out of print. In 1967 it was brought back out by Avon, but is currently out of print again.

Ralph Ellison's *Invisible Man* (1952) produces an image of the Afro-American that challenges those produced by Wright and other naturalists. The novel deals with the initiation rites of its nameless protagonist into a society where he cannot exist and be acknowledged as an individual. The novel transforms most of its characters into the *Other* where they function as markers for the validation of the *Other.* After enduring the battle royal where he acquires his scholarship and briefcase, the nameless protagonist enters a Southern black college to prepare to serve the race. But, he is expelled because out of innocence he takes a white donor to an area of town that is not on the itinerary. The novel chronicles this nameless protagonist's search for understanding and visibility. As he travels throughout the North, he encounters individuals who see him as an *Other* that can validate their own "line" or destiny. As the mad vet points out, the character Norton sees the protagonist only as a marker, a pawn, in executing his destiny. For the young Emerson, the protagonist can validate his liberalism. For Brother Jack, the nameless protagonist exists to embody the "Negro question." Only in the basement where he comes to accept his invisibility can he take refuge from the *Other.*

Ellison's protagonist is sufficiently intelligent to analyze, reject, and search; and Ellison uses him to show the limitations of certain American and Afro-American social and intellectual practices, such as liberalism, Marxism, and nationalism. But although *Invisible Man* produces a different image of the Afro-American, it is unable to produce new definitions and assumptions for its protagonist to use in forging his life. As a result the text ends with the protagonist underground with the promise that he will reemerge.

Invisible Man, at least in intention, is not revolutionary in the sense that Hurston's and Hughes's works are revolutionary. Whereas the latter are trying to strain existing generic techniques in order to talk about an Other, Ellison is reproducing an existential literary experience that is trapped in the discourse that emerged with Sartre and Camus in the 1940s in Europe, and with Dostoyevsky from nineteenth-century Russia. This existential literary discourse concerns intellectual, rational, modern man's alienation from bourgeois society, from the nonrational, spiritual, and mystical dimensions of human existence. Ellison's invisible man, unlike Hurston's Janie Starks, cannot deal with or even envision *different* definitions of reality that are not sanctioned by the dominant society. He must remain underground until the dominant ideological formation produces alternatives.

Invisible Man was received enthusiastically by mainstream critics and reviewers. In the *Saturday Review of Literature* Harvey Webster claimed that Ellison was the first black writer to achieve equality with the best white novelists:

> Many Negro writers of real distinction have emerged in our century: Arna Bontemps, Ann Petry, Chester Himes, Langston Hughes, Gwendolyn Brooks, Richard Wright. But none of them, except, sometimes, Richard Wright has been able to transcend the bitter way of life they are still . . . condemned

to, or to master patiently the intricacies of craftsmanship so that they become the peers of the best white writers of our day. Mr. Ellison has achieved this difficult transcendence. *Invisible Man* is not a great Negro novel; it is a work of art any contemporary writer could point to with pride.[37]

In the *New York Times Book Review,* Wright Morris argues that "*Invisible Man* belongs on the shelf with the classical efforts man has made to chart the river Lethe from its mouth to its source."[38] *Time* magazine calls *Invisible Man* a "remarkable first novel. . . . It makes [Ellison] . . . an unusual writer by any standards."[39]

In examining these reviews we can see again how normative criticism works. The reviewers and critics stress *Invisible Man*'s similarities to other "classical" texts within the literary canon. They praise Ellison for mastering "patiently the intricacies of craftsmanship" and thus becoming the "peer of the best white writers," for not having written a "Negro" novel, and for producing certain aesthetic qualities and adhering to an established definition of the literary experience. *Invisible Man*'s favorable reviews sent signals to other literary institutions. The novel was on bestseller's lists and was awarded the National Book Award. It has remained in print since its publication.

But despite the favorable reviews, its status on the bestseller's lists, and its National Book Award, *Invisible Man* was not automatically included in the traditional American literary canon. Thirty years after its publication its token inclusion in traditional American literature courses still draws attention. Why the historical exclusion from the American literary canon of Afro-American texts such as Toomer's *Cane,* Wright's *Native Son,* Dunbar's *Sports of the Gods,* Demby's *Beetlecreek,* and Ellison's *Invisible Man,* which have been defined as "great" by mainstream critics, reviewers, and literary academies? Why the exclusion of Afro-American texts such as Hurston's *Their Eyes Were Watching God,* Brooks's *Maud Martha,* Chesnutt's *The Marrow of Tradition,* and Wilson's *Our Nig,* which stretch dominant American and Afro-American stereotypes, images, and conventions in an attempt to talk about an *Other* Afro-American? Is the answer to these questions simply intentional, motivated racism, or does the answer lie in the exclusionary nature of the discursive formations (and all discursive formations exclude) of the dominant American ideological apparatus and its literary practices? Some of the exclusion is due to blatant intentional racism. But most of it has to do with the exclusionary nature of the dominant American ideological apparatus, which can be interpreted as racism. Within the ideological apparatus and its literary practices, the Afro-American is defined as an Other who by definition must be subordinated, negated, ignored, or invested with myths and images that integrate him into the "natural" order of things. The subordination or exclusion allows the ideological apparatus to overcome the contradiction the Afro-American represents. To talk of "great" literature, even by Afro-American writers, and to have the Afro-American, who has been subordinated or defined as inferior within the ideological apparatus, as the subject means to challenge those presuppositions, or the discursive formation, upon which the ideological apparatus rests. Thus when Webster defines *Invisible Man* as a "great" novel, he cannot simultaneously see it as a "Negro novel." The two statements are contradictory terms. But, of course, given the nature of the ideological apparatus, *Invisible Man* has to be a "Negro novel." Otherwise, why the disclaimer?

Furthermore, the rigid, dominant labels and stereotypes—such as primitive, exotica, passive victim, etc.—that have historically defined the Afro-American occlude other aspects of the Afro-American. First, the Afro-American does not stand outside the reflexive circuitry of production and reproduction that links together the separate and fragmented pieces of the American social reality. There is no reason to suppose that before the 1960s the Afro-American affirmed only those things that uniquely belonged to him. He also affirmed some of the preferred meanings, values, images, and interpretations—those favored and transmitted through the authorized channels, institutions, and apparatuses—that included him as the Other and, by definition, subordinate. When Afro-American writers such as Chesnutt, Toomer, and Hurston violated or stretched normative literary conventions, images, and stereotypes to produce Afro-American characters whose lived and theoretical concepts of history and self were *different* from the one imposed by the dominant society, their works were either appropriated—thereby effecting certain silences in critical discourse—or ignored. Those Afro-American writers such as Langston Hughes who portrayed the Afro-American as an interpenetration of American and African lives, and therefore questioned certain established labels and stereotypes, were also appropriated—that is, defined by one of the categories ("primitive," etc.) within the ideological apparatus, or excluded.

The exclusionary nature of the dominant ideological apparatus affects the production of Afro-American texts and images. It certifies exceptional texts such as *Invisible Man* and *Native Son* that reproduce established literary conventions and experiences by giving them *token* representation in the canon. To remain in print and to receive some critical acclaim, other Afro-American texts must be promoted by nonhegemonic literary and social movements that have the apparatus such as journals to deem them legitimate. For example, since the seventies, a feminist constellation has exhumed from the literary archives and appropriated texts such as Hurston's *Their Eyes Were Watching God,* Brooks's *Maud Martha,* and Pauline Hopkins's *Contending Forces.* Since the sixties an Afro-American nationalist constellation has appropriated and brought back into print texts such as Dunbar's *The Sport of Gods,* Chesnutt's *The Marrow of Tradition,* and Delaney's *Blake.* Without a nonhegemonic movement of different aesthetic tastes to declare that Afro-American texts such as Demby's *Beetlecreek* possess literary merit, these texts go out of print.

The sixties movements signaled a change in the dominant American ideological apparatus. In their move to delegitimate the ideological apparatus, they produced the context for Afro-American writers to write new kinds of Afro-American texts, to produce new images of the Afro-American, and to enter a new phase of their century-old struggle with dominant American critical practices—mainstream editors, publishers, reviewers, critics, and their assumptions about literature—to determine which images of the Afro-American will appear before the American reading public.

Chapter 3. Sixties' Social Movements, the Literary Establishment, and the Production of the Afro-American Text

During the 1960s Afro-Americans declared war on the social, political, psychological, and cultural institutions and apparatuses within the dominant American ideological apparatus. They argued that these institutions did not contribute to the building of a black nation. Afro-American writers also questioned many of the dominant American literary conventions, assumptions, and practices. Amiri Baraka wanted a literature that accented only that which was uniquely Afro-American. Haki Madhubuti built educational institutions that had Afrikan values. Addison Gayle, Holt Fuller, and Ron Karenga devised a theory of literature, the black aesthetic, that exposed the "enemies" and presented only positive images of the Afro-American.

The preceding chapter was concerned with how the various mainstream institutions within the dominant American literary establishment produced Afro-American texts and Afro-American images before the 1960s, and how Afro-American writers struggled to refute those established myths and images they felt were dehumanizing and debilitating. This chapter is concerned with the sixties' social movements, their effects on the dominant American ideological cultural apparatus, and the production of new Afro-American images and new Afro-American texts.

This chapter assumes that Afro-America, as a result of an enormous social transformation, developed ostensibly as a more visible and sharply defined urban, racial, and cultural group.

This transformation, which resulted from economic modernization in the South and industrial expansion in the North, caused a shift in the labor force and mass migration out of the rural South where the majority of blacks lived until the 1950s. After 1950 a new phenomenon of Afro-American social reality appeared: large urban black populations.

Between World War II and the early 1970s many changes transpired in America. There were large-scale industrialization and urbanization. Advances in technology continued to revolutionize industry and the workplace, and the hegemony of the United States as a world superpower materialized. It is impossible to determine the effects of this technologically transformed society and these new complex societal forces on the Afro-American. But one result is obvious: most blacks acquired a different basis for addressing their existence. New modes of self-expression and new systems of representation began to emerge.

The most far-reaching consequence of this adjustment was the breakdown of traditional authority, as well as the questioning of certain belief structures. The brand of Christianity that was fermented and preached under the slave conditions of the rural South, and that had lasted nearly a hundred years after Emancipation, simply could not have any real relevancy or meaning to the black youth growing up under the complex industrial systems of the urban centers. In short, the influence of the church declined steadily as its administration failed to keep up with the demands and realities of this new urban Afro-American social reality.

The second belief structure to fall asunder, or be seriously undermined, was that of white supremacy. In the late fifties and early sixties the institutionalized racial repression that placed blacks at the bottom of the American economy and denied them full participation in the American society no longer seemed "natural." With the revolution in telecommunication—especially in television—that brought people in the world closer together, and with the return of black soldiers from other parts of the world after World War II where they had experienced "freedom," blacks no longer conceived the world as one where whites had to be on top and blacks on the bottom.

Adding to these underminings of the dominant American ideological apparatus was, by the 1960s, the too obvious discrepancy between the realities of black life and the realities of white
life. Between 1910 and 1950 the number of unskilled workers—
the group to which most urban blacks belonged—declined from
25 million to somewhat under 13 million. By 1962 the number
had plummeted to fewer than 4 million.[1] Although the move
from countryside to city had on the average meant a higher standard of living for blacks (the bottom of the urban-industrial lad-
der is higher than the bottom of the Southern agricultural lad-
der, and when blacks stepped from one to the other, it was a
step up), black unemployment rates doubled those of whites by
the early 1960s.

With the United States at one of its most prosperous moments
in its history, the increasing economic disparity between blacks
and whites became unavoidably apparent. These economic discrepancies made discontent inevitable. "Economic crisis tendency," argues Habermas, asserts "itself as a social crisis and leads
to political struggles."[2] The social discontent was signified by
urban race riots and rebellions. There was Watts in 1965,
Newark in 1966, and Detroit in 1967. These riots and rebellions,
along with economic discrepancies and more available information, heightened the civil rights and black power struggles and
continued to undermine and bring into question the authority
and legitimacy of the dominant American ideological apparatus.

Concurrent with the early stages of the civil rights movement,
which had challenged successfully in the courts the legality of
certain laws barring blacks from full participation in the dominant American society's institutions and practices, were other
fermenting social developments that would question and undermine some of the moral and political practices within the ideological apparatus. First, the economic prosperity in the United
States in the 1950s produced a large suburban white leisure middle class. The white youth segment of this middle class was a
part of the rise of the large state universities and mass education. Hence lay a seed for the student movement in the 1960s.

Moreover, in the 1950s the domination of the political arena
by Cold War politics had meant repression of political dissent.

The fear of Soviet aggression and the threat of Communist expansion produced a climate of intense repression, which caused censorship within the major institutions and apparatuses. Debate of domestic and foreign policies in the public arena was monitored closely, and the normative platform had a narrow range. Too much deviation from a prescribed set of assumptions landed one before the House Committee on Un-American Activities. With this repression, many Americans became silent and accepted the facade of business as usual.

In addition, the 1950s was a time of enormous sexual repression. Sexuality was confined to married couples and the bedroom. Sexuality of children was denied; therefore, they were forbidden to talk about it. All gestures, symbols, and manifestations of human sexuality were repressed. This silence on sexuality produced illegitimate sexualities in the brothels. Outside of these places, modern puritanism imposed its taboo, repression, and negation.

In the early 1960s the fermenting civil rights movement produced the options for disenchanted and repressed groups—blacks, Asians, Chicanos, Native Americans, students, antiwar activists, and sexual liberators—to channel their aggressions and frustrations and to form American social movements which would challenge the legitimacy of the dominant American ideological apparatus. These American social movements caused a crisis in the dominant society's sociocultural system. Explaining this crisis, Jürgen Habermas writes:

> We have to reckon with cultural crisis tendencies when the normative structures change, according to their inherent logic, in such a way that the complementarity between the requirements of the state apparatus and the occupational system, on the one hand, and the interpreted needs and legitimate expectations of members of society, on the other, is disturbed. Legitimation crises result from a need for legitimation that arises from changes in the political system.[3]

These American social movements of the sixties formulated a challenge to the dominant American ideological apparatus, moved to undermine its process of normalization, challenged its principle of unity and cohesion, exposed its constraints and limitations, and contradicted its myth of an American consensus.

In straining, stretching, parodying, and violating the social, cultural, political, and literary institutions and practices within the dominant ideological apparatus, these American social movements moved to its marginality. In this marginality, this raw state, the Afro-American, along with other repressed social entities, was able to assess his situation and history from a context that had not been colonized by the dominant ideological apparatus.

To violate normative social, political, and cultural practices, these American social movements accented differences. For example, Afro-Americans began using cultural forms, images, symbols, and myths—either exhumed from the African and Afro-American historical past or developed in the present—that were different from those of the dominant ideological apparatus. Afro-Americans began to invent, or exhume from the historical past, new ways of relating—calling each other brother and sister; new social relations—accenting a communal and cooperative approach to family life; new types of nonexploitive values different from those appropriated by the dominant society. They began inventing new types of behavior and new systems of representations—new forms of dress, speech, and style. The Afro-American invented, or exhumed from the historical past, new types of interchanges between individuals that were neither the same as, nor superimposed on, existing dominant American cultural forms and myths. This stress on differences defamiliarized the dominant American society's practices, thereby showing the American public, and especially Afro-Americans, that what had been presented as "natural" was in fact a construct, a production.

The dominant ideological apparatus had to respond to these American social movements of the sixties. To survive, it had to make concessions; it also had to maintain itself. Political, social, educational, and cultural institutions and practices within the ideological apparatus became more flexible and expansive. The political arena opened up to include black elected officials. Blacks began to form a presence in state legislatures. Colleges and universities enrolled larger numbers of black students. The corporate and business world and the media institutions became more sensitive to the historical exclusion of blacks and other minorities.

Within the cultural apparatus, the literary institutions—publishing houses, editors, review journals and magazines, granting and awarding agencies, English departments—became more sensitive to the exclusion of Afro-American literature, other minority literatures, and women's literature. With the establishment of Afro-American and other minorities' studies programs and departments, the lives and histories of Afro-Americans and other minorities in general and their literatures in particular were acknowledged. Major publishing houses began publishing more than two "Negro" novels a year, and they came to see Afro-America as constituting a specific audience. There was a tremendous upsurge in Chicano, Native American, and Asian-American poetry and fiction. Talented minority writers such as James Welch, Leslie Silko, Tomas Rivera, Rudolfo A. Anaya, John Okada, Lawson Inada, Maxine Kingston, Frank Chin, and others were able to be published by mainstream publishing houses.

Afro-American poetry, drama, and fiction mushroomed in ways never seen before in American literary history. The movement was not concentrated in one city, as the Harlem Renaissance was in the 1920s, but was dispersed throughout the country. Afro-American texts were more readily discussed and reviewed in the pages of several major review journals and magazines. Between 1968 and 1973 it was not unusual to read reviews by Addison Gayle, Saunders Redding, Julius Lester, and Toni Morrison in the *New York Times Book Review* and the *Book World* of the *Washington Post.* Public, college, and university libraries also purchased Afro-American texts and developed Afro-American collections. Bookstores began to stock Afro-American and other minority texts, and English departments, due to an elective system that dominated the humanities in the late sixties and early seventies, offered courses in Afro-American and other minority literatures.

Some literary critics and reviewers become more conscious of the ideological biases they brought to Afro-American literature. Some white critics admitted openly the differences that existed between blacks and whites, and that perhaps they were not best qualified to serve as authorities on black literature. In their introduction to *The Politics of Literature,* Louis Kampf and Paul Lauter indicate the need for blacks to work separately and discuss how that need "has its source in the sharp differences of black and white social experience in the United States."[4] More important, perhaps, Lauter's remark shows the constraints of normative criticism. It brings to the forefront of the American literary scene the reality of literature as having cultural and ideological functions.

In addition, the presence of Afro-American and other minority texts in the universities, in the libraries, on the pages of some of America's major literary journals, and on editors' and publishers' desks sent signals to other institutions. Book circuits began including minority texts, and granting agencies began to fund minority scholars, creative artists, and conferences. Minority writers were considered by national awarding agencies. N. Scott Momaday, a Kiowa Indian, was awarded the Pulitzer Prize for his novel *House Made of Dawn.* Audre Lorde, Nikki Giovanni, and others were nominated for the National Book Award. Many of the sixties minority poets—Ethridge Knight, Alice Walker, Lucille Clifton, Carolyn Rodgers, Gary Soto, Ai, Lawson Inada, and others—received monies from the Guggenheim and other prestigious foundations.

The Rockefeller and Ford foundations began supporting minority scholars and artists. Both foundations established graduate-level and postdoctoral fellowships for minority-oriented research. And by the mid-seventies the National Endowment for the Humanities—which has a ripple effect on university hiring and tenure and on the kinds of research undertaken by scholars seeking support—under Joe Duffy subsidized different and innovative research, including ethnic and feminist studies. In becoming a symbol of pluralism in generating differences in the seventies, the National Endowment for the Humanities empowered groups that had been regarded as extraneous to "serious" scholarship.[5]

In its expansion, the dominant ideological apparatus in the seventies permitted a kind of pluralism to emerge. The sense of an Anglo-centered cultural system that served as a "universal" model for correcting and measuring the worth of all cultural objects gave way to a diversity that began to embrace America in all her complexities and differences. Blacks, Asians, Chicanos, Native Americans, and European ethnic groups began to accent their differences from the dominant Anglo culture and began establishing different criteria for determining the worth of their own literatures. In short, they began to address the political and ideological nature of literature.

This expansion of the dominant society's institutions and practices, coupled with the rise of independent black publishing houses, journals, and magazines—Jihads, Broadside Press, Third World Press, the Third Press, Vintage Press, Yardbird Press, *Black Books Bulletin, Black World, Freedomways,* the *Black Scholar,* the *Journal of Black Studies, Black American Literature Forum,* and others—caused a change in the literary and ideological forces that produced Afro-American texts. It gave Afro-American writers, perhaps for the first time in American history, the opportunity to write for black audiences of similar ideological persuasions. This freedom, along with the materials and perspectives produced by the sixties social movements, allowed Afro-American writers to write new kinds of texts. Some—such as Alice Walker, Albert Murray, Ernest J. Gaines, Toni Cade Bambara, Ishmael Reed, and Toni Morrison—rummaged the American, African, and Afro-American historical past for the "stuff," the spiritual, psychological, and historical forms and myths, that could give the contemporary Afro-American a greater sense of his being, that could validate, make coherent, and give meaning and history to his lived experiences.

Within these emerging discursive formations—cultural nationalism, feminism, omni-Americanism—Afro-American writers could continue to burst asunder more forcefully the dominant passive, safe, and one-dimensional images and stereotypes and produce new archetypes that would serve their own ideological needs. The matriarchal and wench stereotypes of Mitchell's *Gone With the Wind* and Faulkner's *The Sound and the Fury* could become popular heroines in Gaines's *The Autobiography of Miss Jane Pittman.* The stifled and stunted stereotypes of Jean

Wheeler Smith's "Frankie Mae," the tragic mulatto stereotypes of Nella Larsen's Helga Crane in *Quicksand* (1928) and Clare Kendry in *Passing* (1929) were allowed to become figures with options, making decisions about their lives, and exploring the complex aspects of their sexuality in the work of seventies black women writers. Ntozake Shange's *For Colored Girls* and Gayl Jones's *Corregidora* strain the dominant wench stereotype of the black woman to present black women characters who expose aspects of their sexuality along with a kind of historical oppression that had never appeared in Afro-American fiction. Toni Morrison's characters Sula and Nel in *Sula* and Toni Cade Bambara's Sweet Pea, Pot Limit, and Sylvia in "Medley" stretch the bitch stereotype and present women characters who exhibit a healthy female support system that has been omitted in Afro-American texts. Paule Marshall's Reena in "Reena" and Alice Walker's Meridian Hill in *Meridian* violate the dumb black woman stereotype and show female protagonists who display a certain political sophistication and personal conviction that are new to the pages of American and Afro-American fiction. The sixties social movements produced the discursive formations for these excluded images and stereotypes of the black women to emerge.

In releasing the Afro-American mind and spirit from the manacles of the dominant American ideological apparatus, the sixties produced the discursive formations for invisible men to emerge from underground and for the Bigger Thomases to discern just what kinds of native sons they really wanted to be. Ellison's invisible man had to remain underground, despite the fact that he possessed the intelligence and awareness to envision a new discursive formation, because extratextual discursive formations had not been produced. As a result of the sixties, the nameless protagonist can emerge in a discursive formation in which he can define himself.

The invisible man, along with the docile and passive images of the Afro-American male in the works of Page and Harris, Twain's *Huckleberry Finn,* Stowe's *Uncle Tom's Cabin,* Van Vechten's *Nigger Heaven,* and Dunbar's *The Fanatics,* emerges and begins to exercise new options in the work of Afro-

American writers of the 1970s. In Ernest Gaines's "The Sky is Grey" the young black male questions "the world . . . with cold logic." When he says that the "wind is pink" and that the "grass is black," he exhibits knowledge and understanding that violate existing discursive knowledge. He knows that everything, including language, is a contrivance, or is discursive. In Wesley Brown's *Tragic Magic,* Melvin Ellington knows that the dominant definition of manhood is a limited, dehumanizing stereotype that he must violate. Other Afro-American texts—such as George Cain's *Blueschild Baby,* Toni Cade Bambara's *The Salt Eaters,* William Melvin Kelley's *A Different Drummer,* John O. Killen's *And Then We Heard the Thunder,* John A. Williams's *Captain Blackman,* and Ishmael Reed's *Mumbo Jumbo*—present characters who enable us to see the constraints and limitations of dominant American literary conventions and stereotypes of the Afro-American. Their characters understand the images, definitions, and conventions that have been fed the Afro-American for three hundred years in the name of universality and naturalness. They are all engaged in a struggle, personal and political, to produce discursive formations where they will be normative.

Some of the above-mentioned writers such as Clarence Major, Ishmael Reed, and Toni Cade Bambara realized that the English language and dominant generic techniques are products of the dominant ideological apparatus. They realized that the novel form serves as a vehicle for the winning and shaping of the consent of the ideological apparatus. Therefore, in their attempts to name other kinds of intelligences—Afro-American prediscursive and presystematic developments—that lay beyond the discursive formation of the ideological apparatus, these writers first had to defamiliarize the "naturalness" of established genres and languages by violating, breaking with, parodying, or playing on those conventions. They had to stretch the English language to its raw state, its exteriority.

Mumbo Jumbo is Ishmael Reed's attempt to write about a spiritual system, "Jes Grew," from the Afro-American historical past. His first task here was to expose the constraints of the traditional novel form. Then he had to make the English language incorporate categories, experiences, and concepts that exist outside its discursive formation (or its linguistic structures). For example, to allow the English language and the text to speak about "jes grew" and "mumbo jumbo," Reed interrupts the narrative. He uses the *American Heritage Dictionary of the English Language* to define "mumbo jumbo": "[Mandingo *ma-ma-gyo-mbo,* 'magician who makes the troubled spirits of ancestors to away'; *ma-ma,* grandmother + *gyo,* trouble + *mbo,* to leave]."[6] He uses James Weldon Johnson's *The Book of American Negro Poetry* to define "jes grew": " . . . we appropriated about the last one of the 'jes grew' songs. It was a song which had been sung for years all through the South. The words were unprintable, but the tune was irresistible, and belonged to nobody."[7] Reed further violates the expected linear sense of time by presenting sequences in nonchronological order. The reader gets the effects of "jes grew" before he is informed of its origins. Reed breaks with and parodies familiar expectations and conventions. For example, he presents chapter one before he gives the title of the novel; he uses one-paragraph chapters. He uses pictures and draws figures to convey graphic messages and images, rather than written descriptions. When Earline shows Papa LaBas an invitation to a Chitterling Switch, the text draws the invitation.

After forcing the reader to admit that the literary text is a production with certain expected conventions, Reed proceeds to defamiliarize the dominant ideological apparatus and Western civilization. He exposes satirically the various strategies used by the various discourses—educational institutions, legal practices, the military, the media, the government—within the ideological apparatus to exclude the Afro-American, the Other. He shows how the historical, sociological, and psychological discourses are not innocent, but function to reproduce the ideological apparatus. He shows how Freud works within the discursive formation of Western rationalism, refusing to hear about the spiritual and nonrational from Papa LaBas. In addition, *Mumbo Jumbo* shows those historical moments—the 1890s, 1920s, and 1960s—when Jes Grew (which "knows no class no race no consciousness. It is self-propagating and you can never tell when it will hit") moved to undermine the discursive practices within the ideological apparatus.

In their violation of dominant literary practices and generic techniques, these texts of the 1960s and 1970s placed themselves in that Afro-American tradition—including Chesnutt's *The Marrow of Tradition,* Bontemps's *Black Thunder,* Hurston's *Their Eyes Were Watching God*—whose authors understood the constraints of these dominant literary practices. Moreover, black and women critics of the decade, unlike their predecessors, no longer accepted normative criticism as natural. Black cultural nationalist and feminist critical practices established their own aesthetic standards and criteria, different from those of the dominant American literary practices, for judging and assessing the worth and value of Afro-American and feminist texts. They countered the appropriation of certain black and feminist texts and maintained before the American literary community what Fredric Jameson describes as "essential polemic and subversive strategies."[8]

The American movements of the sixties produced the options for three dominant Afro-American discourses to reemerge and reestablish themselves. Historically, black nationalism as a discourse in the United States can be traced to the first slave conspiracy in 1526. Since that time the black nationalist discourse has informed a nationalist Afro-American literary tradition which begins with Delany's *Blake, or The Huts of America* (1895) and Sutton Griggs's *Imperium in Imperio* (1902). The tradition enjoyed a renaissance in the 1920s and again in the 1960s.

Feminism as a discourse in black women writings and speeches dates back to Sojourner Truth and Francis Harper who were very active in the women's suffrage movement of the nineteenth century. As a literary discourse, feminism informs Hurston's *Their Eyes Were Watching God* (1937). It reemerged in the early 1970s with more vigor, commitment, sophistication, and political acumen.

Finally, omni-Americanism, or the focus on culture rather than race, as an Afro-American discourse traces its beginnings to early America. It emerged as a category for those Afro-Americans who embraced uncritically the values of the dominant society, or who felt that narrow racial categories did not explain all of their lived experiences. With Frederick Douglass and Booker T. Washington, it dominated Afro-American politics in the nineteenth century. As a literary discourse, it informed William Wells Brown's *Clotel* (1853), Frank Webb's *The Garies and Their Friends* (1857), Pauline Hopkins's *Contending Forces* (1899), James Weldon Johnson's *The Autobiography of an Ex-Coloured Man* (1912), and other Afro-American texts that deal with the interracial Afro-American imprisoned in inadequate labels, or that embrace values of the dominant culture. Omni-Americanism mushroomed in the poetry of Melvin Tolson and Robert Hayden and in Ralph Ellison's *Invisible Man* in the 1950s.

Since the sixties movements produced the discursive formations for the Afro-American to redefine self and history, the most crucial question confronting the Afro-American writer of the decade was: what constitutes the American and Afro-American historical past. These sixties discourses allowed new myths about, or representations of, the American and Afro-American historical past to emerge. The cultural nationalist discourse was triggered by the dominant American ideological apparatus, the literary practices it appropriates, and the Afro-American assimilationalist discourse of the 1950s with its exclusion of the Afro-American heroic past. In an interview with John O'Brien, Ernest Gaines echoes this nationalist sentiment:

> ... when I first started reading I wanted to read about my people in the South, and the white writers whom I had read did not put my people into books the way that I knew them. When I did not find my people in the Southern writers, I started reading books about the peasantry in other places. . . . This led me to reading the writers of other countries. Then in some way I went into the Russians and I liked what they were doing with their stories on the peasantry; the peasants were real human beings, whereas in the fiction of American writers, especially Southern writers, they were caricatures of human beings, they were clowns.[9]

The cultural nationalist discourse produced historical texts such as Gaines's *The Autobiography of Miss Jane Pittman* and Alex

Haley's *Roots* that emphasized the heroic qualities or tradition from the Afro-American historical past.

The omni-American discourse reemerged also in reaction to the cultural nationalist's and the dominant society's discursive formations that omitted the existence of the American and Afro-American who are products of culture as much as, if not more than, of race. Ralph Ellison argues, "The 'Black Aesthetic' crowd buys the idea of total cultural separation between blacks and whites, suggesting that we've been left out of the mainstream. But when we examine American music and literature in terms of its themes, symbolism, rhythms, tonalities, idioms and images it is obvious that those rejected 'Negroes' have been a vital part of the mainstream and were from the beginning."[10] In another reaction, James Alan McPherson writes:

> It [omni-Americanism] is . . . a product of culture and not of race. And achieving it will require that one be conscious of America's culture and the complexity of all its people. . . .
> Why, for example, should black Americans raised in the Southern culture *not* find that some of their responses are geared to country music? How else, except in terms of cultural diversity, am I to account for the white friend in Boston who taught me much of what I know about black American music? Or the white friend in Virginia who . . . knows more about black American folklore than most black people? Or the possibility that many black people in Los Angeles have been just as much influenced by Hollywood's "star system" of the forties and fifties as they have been by society's response to the color of their skins?[11]

The omni-American discourse produced texts, such as Albert Murray's *Train Whistle Guitar*, Leon Forrest's *There Is a Tree More Ancient Than Eden*, and Al Young's *Who is Angelina?*, that define the historical past by cultural forms.

Later, in the early seventies, feminists or black women produced representations of the historical past that show the historical oppression of black women and show that black women, underneath one-dimensional stereotypes, are complex human beings. The feminist discourse was triggered by the dominant

American society's, the black cultural nationalist's, and white women's representations of the historical past that excluded the black woman. Reacting to dominant literary practices, Pat Crutchfield Exum comments, "Few American writers have spoken for the black community as a whole, and even fewer have spoken for the silent black woman. Negative stereotypes of black womanhood have generally been used to glorify the goodness, the pureness, and innocence of the white 'lady.' Wench, matriarch, mammy: these are the images that have been imposed upon her, and her complexities and truths—simple or complex —have been buried under them."[12] Reacting to the literary practices of cultural nationalism, Ntozake Shange concludes, "I guess I've been in every black nationalist movement in the country, and I found that the flaw in the nationalists' dream was that they didn't treat women right."[13] Finally, reverberating against white women's exclusion of black women, Alice Walker says that "white feminists revealed themselves as incapable as white and black men of comprehending blackness and feminism in the same body, not to mention with the same imagination. . . . In any case, it is not my child who tells me: I have no femaleness white women must affirm. Not my child who says: I have no rights black men must respect."[14] This feminist discourse produced texts such as Toni Morrison's *The Bluest Eye* and *Sula,* Alice Walker's *The Third Life of Grange Copeland* and *The Color Purple,* Ntozake Shange's *For Colored Girls,* and Gayl Jones's *Corregidora* and *Eva's Man* that produced new myths about black women in the historical past.

The Afro-American texts produced by this seventies discourse function to give meaning and history, and to validate and make coherent the strivings and yearnings of those Americans who embrace feminism because it explains certain lived experiences. These texts develop value in accordance with "particular criteria and in light of given purposes."[15] The problems and issues explored in these texts and the resolutions they offer function as indices and cultural messages. In short, as a collection of texts that emphasize similar human experiences and categories from the past and that provide similar resolutions, they function as a social institution.

The next four chapters will examine four texts—Ernest J. Gaines's *The Autobiography of Miss Jane Pittman,* Alice Walker's *The Third Life of Grange Copeland,* Albert Murray's *Train Whistle Guitar,* and Toni Morrison's *Sula*—from three sixties and seventies discourses, delineated above, to show how they produce different representations of the same American and Afro-American historical past, and to explain the significance of that production. Second, these chapters will examine how these texts strain the ability of generic techniques to effect a closure within their discursive formations, and how that strain reveals the ideological effect of generic systems. Finally, these four chapters will examine how these texts are appropriated not only by the dominant American literary practices but by the literary practices of their respective discursive formations.

Chapter 4. History, the Black Nationalist Discourse, and *The Autobiography of Miss Jane Pittman*

Ernest J. Gaines's *The Autobiography of Miss Jane Pittman* was published in 1971 at the culmination of the black nationalist movement of the 1960s, and it gives meaning and history to the Afro-American who needs to make sense out of a historical past—slavery, pain, suffering, injustice—that had been excluded by dominant American historical texts and myths. To produce this nationalist historical past in *Miss Jane Pittman,* Gaines strains dominant American myths and stereotypes, reproduced in the works of American writers such as Thomas Nelson Page, Harris S. Edwards, Mark Twain, Harriet Stowe, and William Faulkner, that portray the Afro-American as passive, as a "caricature" of a human being, as a "clown," and that portray the black woman as a wench, a matriarch, or a bitch.[1] *Miss Jane Pittman* produces an American and Afro-American historical past that, Gaines says, puts "my people" in it the "way I knew them."[2] It produces a historical past that shows the courage, strength, and dignity of the Afro-American. In an interview with Ruth Laney, Gaines discusses the source of his characters' strength and dignity:

> She was my great-aunt, and she never walked a day in her life. She'd crawl over the floor as a child six or seven months old might crawl over the floor. But her arms were very strong. She'd cook for us. . . . She could make bread, bake our bread. . . . She could wash our clothes. . . . She could sew our

clothes. . . . Besides that, she used to get into the little garden
to work among her vegetables. . . . Other times, she would
crawl into our back yard to pick up pecans. . . . This is the
kind of courage that I tried to give Miss Jane. . . .[3]

Black nationalism, which emphasizes the courage and dignity
of Afro-Americans both past and present, informs the discursive
formation of *Miss Jane Pittman.* Three elements form the basis
of sixties black nationalism. The most essential and elementary
component is the notion of unity or solidarity. Historically, there
has been a tendency among blacks in the United States, with
notable exceptions, to view the United States as an individualistic society when in fact it has always been a country in which
groups (racial, ethnic, class, etc.) have used unity as a means of
advancement for their members.[4] The notion of the melting pot
was based on the belief that members of diverse groups coming
to America would abandon their cultural heritage and would embrace the dominant society's values, traditions, and myths.
While this pattern held true to a degree for many, especially im-
migrants from northern Europe, it did not hold true for blacks
who were denied not only the right to participate freely in the
dominant culture but also the opportunity to practice their African cultures. In order to move into America's mainstream institutions and practices, blacks needed the force of unity. It is
through black unity, argues Amiri Baraka, that blacks will
achieve "power, black power, for black people to control our
lives, to build our own cities, and re-create the glorious civiliza-
tions of our history."[5]

A second major element in sixties black nationalism is the
pride in cultural heritage that takes on added significance for Afro-Americans because of the widespread American practice of
deprecating African and Afro-American cultural objects. Black
nationalism instills in Afro-Americans pride in their African and
Afro-American cultural heritages and in their common grief in
suffering. Noted historian Eric Foner defines black nationalism
not only as a rejection by blacks of a society that has rejected
them, but also as "an affirmation of the unique traditions, values, and cultural heritage of black Americans."[6]

Third and finally, black nationalists maintain that in order for Afro-Americans to liberate themselves from oppression, some degree of autonomy from the dominant society is essential. While differences of opinion exist as to the extent to which autonomy is necessary (ranging from local community control to the formation of a separate nation-state), there is a general agreement that, given the nature of American society, some degree of autonomy is necessary for self-determination.

Black nationalism informed *Miss Jane Pittman*'s discursive formation by causing Gaines to select certain historical facts and to exclude others—thereby revealing the text's ideological consequences or generic systems. *Miss Jane Pittman*'s discursive formation, its generic techniques, and the literary conventions it needed to effect a closure determined how it would be appropriated by dominant American and Afro-American reviewers and critics.

Self-consciously revealing its intention and its "rules of formation," the introduction to *Miss Jane Pittman* indicates that the text will produce a particular representation of the Afro-American historical past. This is signified when the narrator acknowledges the need to impose a structure, a meaning, an interpretation, on the mass of random materials about the historical past he has received from Miss Jane and the people of her community:

> There were times when I thought the narrative was taking ridiculous directions. Miss Jane would talk about one thing one day and the next day she would talk about something else totally different. If I were bold enough to ask: "But what about such and such a thing?" she would look at me incredulously and say, "Well, what about it?" . . . And Mary would say, "But What?" I would say, "I just wanted to tie up all the loose ends." Mary would say, "Well, you don't tie up all the loose ends all the time. And if you got to change her way of telling it, you tell it yourself. . . . "
>
> I could not possibly put down on paper everything that Miss Jane and the others said on the tape during those eight or nine months. Much of it was too repetitious and did not follow a

single direction. What I have tried to do here was not write everything, but in essence everything that was said.[7]

In the exchange with Mary, the teacher/narrator learns an invaluable lesson about reality, existence, and meaning and how they are formed: they are discursive formations comprised of groups of relations that form determinations that permit and exclude. To write Miss Jane's life story, or any story, the narrator has to impose a structure.

The nature of the teacher/narrator's intention is shown further in the conversation with Mary:

> "What you want know about Miss Jane for?" Mary said.
> "I teach history," I said. "I'm sure her life's story can help me explain things to my students."
> "What's wrong with them books you already got?" Mary said.
> "Miss Jane is not in them," I said.[8]

This conversation shows clearly that there are other representations of the American and Afro-American historical past that exist outside the text. But *Miss Jane Pittman*'s discursive formation is attempting to represent these other representations as exclusions.

Miss Jane Pittman, the story of a 110-year-old black woman who gives an account of her life and the life of Afro-America from slavery to the 1960s, is divided into four books. Each book is related to the others in that it repeats certain discursive facts and stereotypes with the intention of generating what Foucault calls an "enunciation"—the object or statement of discourse—within the text. The historical moments that the text emphasizes are all eruptive or transitional moments—moments when individuals are forced to make decisions about their lives. *Miss Jane Pittman* is biased toward those individuals who act, those who make the decision to move, to take a risk, to explore the unknown and therefore to learn about their strengths and capabilities. In an article entitled "Idea and Form in Literature," Georg Lukács argues that the truth of the driving forces of social development must be given in the form of action, that this truth of social development can be measured by the destinies of the individual: "The world of people, their subjective sensations and thoughts show their truthfulness or falsity, their sincerity or mendacity, their greatness or narrowness of mind. . . . Only through deeds do people become interesting to one another. Only through deeds do people become worthy of poetic portrayal. The basic features of the human character can be revealed only through deeds and actions in human practice."[9]

The four books of *Miss Jane Pittman* concern those facts and statements from the American and Afro-American historical past which have "deeds and actions," those individuals who struggle against the existing social structures in an attempt to produce others. Book I, "The War Years," details the struggle of certain freed slaves to define new modes of existence. When the Emancipation Proclamation is passed abolishing slavery, the slaves are confronted with the difficult and frightening task of deciding what to do with their lives. Will they remain with the past? Will they shape the future? Will they reestablish old patterns in new guises, or will they seek new existences? The young, Jane among them, show a rebellious spirit. They break "cotton stalks," change their names, and strive for new physical existences in the North. The elders, whose lives are tied to the past and the status quo, are more reluctant to embrace these radical changes.

Miss Jane embodies this rebellious new spirit; she decides to act. She changes her name from Ticey to Jane and, defying the advice of the elders, embarks upon a questing odyssey North:

> Before the master could open his mouth, I said: "Where North at? Point to it. I'll show y'all where to go."
> The driver said: "Shut up. You ain't nothing but trouble. I ain't had nothing but trouble out you since you come in that field."
> "If I ain't nothing but trouble, you ain't nothing but Nothing," I said.
> And the next thing I knowed, my mouth was numb and I was laying down there on the ground. . . .
> I jumped up from there and sunk my teeth in that nigger's hand.[10]

Miss Jane's odyssey takes her throughout the state of Louisiana, blindly in search of freedom and the North. In these travels, Miss Jane encounters an array of discursive stereotypes, stereotypes that have become a part of codified and accepted definitions of the American and Afro-American historical past. There are the patrollers—"poor white trash"—who find and return the runaway slaves to the masters, the submissive uncle tom driver who "goes where us misses tell us to go." There is the rude white lady who expresses the hatred some whites have toward blacks for causing "all this trouble, all this ravishing."[11]

In her travels Miss Jane also encounters the hunter who has a friendly face and many words of wisdom. In scolding Jane for her uninformed quests to go North, he says,

> "But they had left out just like you, a few potatoes and another old dress. No map, no guide, no nothing. Like freedom was a place coming to meet them half way. Well, it ain't coming to meet you. And it might not be there when you get there, either."[12]

She also encounters the old white man from the North—"not kind, but not mean"—who offers Jane and Ned, Big Laura's son, food and gives them direction to Ohio.

But Big Laura, who represents stamina and courage and who is excluded from dominant myths about the American and Afro-American historical past, is the most dominant figure in Book I. Big Laura initiates the heroic growth and travels of Miss Jane and Ned. Viewed as a leader of the freed slaves, she is portrayed as being physically and mentally stronger than human: "She was big just like her name say, and she was tough as any man I ever seen. She could plow, chop wood, cut and load much cane as any man on the place."[13] Symbolically, Big Laura has to die, for her strength and courage are immediate threats to the normative social structure. The flint and iron, which Jane and Ned guard and protect tenaciously, embody and symbolize the black strength, courage, and pride which Big Laura and other defiant blacks represent.

From the description of linguistic structures, we can identify the formation of discursive facts and categories—the objects of the discourse—in the text. Big Laura, as a heroic and courageous Afro-American from the historical past who is murdered because she does not accept the ruling social order's legitimacy, becomes a discursive fact that forms within the text. Book I also gives full portraits of Jane and Ned as they exhibit their natural intelligence and stamina, to find their way to freedom. Ned and Jane as courageous youths become a discursive category that forms in the text. A violent, oppressive force, manifested in Book I as ruling white males, within the American historical past forms another discursive category. As discursive facts and categories, these significations have limits and functions within the text. They are constrained by the complex group of relations that comprises the text's discursive formation.

Book II, "Reconstruction," reproduces other stereotypes and conventions—the arrival of Northerners in the South, politicians who are wooing black votes for the Republican Party, the rise of terrorist groups (White Brotherhood, KKK) the exodus of blacks from the South to the North, the Secesh's regaining of land and power in the South, and the removal of the Yankee soldiers. Again, as in Book I, the text produces discursive stereotypes that are a part of certain codified definitions of the American and Afro-American historical past.

But as in Book I the historical characters and situations that receive emphasis are men who are courageous and daring, who are willing to die in order to be men—discursive facts which are omitted from established representations of the American and Afro-American historical past. Joe Pittman's struggle to conquer nature and thereby prove his manhood is manifested in his conquest of the stallion. In his determination to capture the wild stallion, he expresses the courage of a readiness to die. When Miss Jane tries to prevent his actions, he tells her that every man signs a contract at birth where he accepts death as the basic condition of life. If a man's life is to have any substantive meaning, he must live it doing his best at what he does best regardless of the danger or consequences. Explaining Joe Pittman's motive for risking death in his determination to break horses, the voodoo woman says, " . . . man is put here to die. From the day he is born him and death take off for that red string. But he never wins, he don't even tie. So the next best thing, do what you can with the little time the Lord spares you. Most men feel they ought to spend them few years proving they men."[14] Like Big Laura, Joe Pittman is another example of the courageous and daring Afro-American who is destroyed by enormous odds. Joe Pittman's struggle with the stallion in Book II functions analogously with Big Laura's fire in the swamp. Each is asserting the black presence courageously against a world that would destroy that presence. Joe Pittman repeats the courageous discursive fact in the text.

But with Joe Pittman, we can discern a correlation between the courageous discursive facts within the text. Joe Pittman symbolizes the emergence of an Afro-American who, in accepting the possibility of death, gains freedom and respect. The arrangement of discursive facts in Book II leads the reader to believe that had Joe Pittman not dared, Ned Douglass would not have acquired the courage he needed. Joe Pittman does not defeat death, Jerry Bryant argues, he defeats the fear of it.[15]

This same book repeats the courageous Afro-American discursive fact in Ned Douglass. Ned has to leave the South because his work with the committee is perceived by whites as a threat to the dominant power structure. After acquiring an education, Ned returns South to preach the social gospel of his namesake, Frederick Douglass. To spread the gospel effectively, Ned builds a school. But, in truth, Ned returns to die, for his strength, courage, determination, and knowledge pose an immediate threat to the existing social structure. As in the case of Big Laura, it is impossible for one person, working alone, to alter a system. Therefore the system crushes him to protect itself. It uses Ned's death as a warning to others who would dare follow in his path.

But with the repetition of the courageous and daring Afro-American discursive fact in Ned Douglass, we discern further correlations between discursive facts, categories, and stereotypes in the text. First, the nature of the oppression shifts from the natural to the social. Joe Pittman's struggle is largely *individual;* he is struggling against nature. Ned's struggle is for black people and against the social order. Unlike Book I where only Ned and Jane are affected by the murder of Big Laura, Book II shows a large section of the ostensible passive black community responding to Ned's murder.

Ned's deeds and actions cause the community to act. The community's response to Ned's murder makes him appear supernatural, Christ-like. Ned's blood does not vanish from the ground "for years and years." His body is brought home on top of a load of lumber and those pieces of wood which are "spotted" with blood are especially prized. In response to Ned's death, Miss Jane and the community finish building the school, which shows that they are learning the value of conserving an unstable past on which to build a viable future.[16] Where Big Laura's murder goes mostly unnoticed in Book I, Ned's murder in Book II awakens the community.

In emphasizing the repetition of the discursive facts of youthful rebellion, courageous and daring Afro-Americans, the repressive natural and social forces that become lethal to heroic Afro-Americans, and the Afro-American community's awakening as a result of this repression, Book II allows the reader to discern *Miss Jane Pittman*'s rules of formation, to establish the conditions for existence of its discursive facts and stereotypes, the order of their successive appearances, their assignable positions within the text, and their correlations with each other. The discursive fact of the repressive force, whether natural or social, and the stereotype of the passive black community function to emphasize the enormous odds the courageous and daring Afro-American must work against. In fact, the repressive odds are so enormous that they destroy the bold and assertive characters like Big Laura, Joe Pittman, and Ned Douglass. The bold and assertive characters, who receive greater emphasis and more textual space, struggle with grace against the repressive forces—thereby showing their courage, dignity, and strength. Ned's persistence in teaching the "gospel" despite threats on his life demonstrates his sincere determination, dignity, and courage. The repeated destruction of the courageous Afro-American allows gradually for the community to learn from its history.

The arrangement and correlations of these discursive facts and stereotypes enable *Miss Jane Pittman* to make a point about the American and Afro-American historical past that is *different* from those made by dominant American discursive formations: that the Afro-American historical past possesses courageous and daring individuals who struggled against the dominant society and who would die rather than accept the oppression of the ruling social order as normative.

In making this point, *Miss Jane Pittman* repeats its discursive facts and stereotypes. Book III, "The Plantation," concerns the personal journey of Miss Jane as she is transformed from a passive observer to a courageous participant. She moves to the Samson Plantation where she does field work. There she submerges herself totally into the life and rituals of the common people. She joins the local church—"after Ned was killed I knowed I had nothing else in the world but the Lord," she explains. She grows to love baseball and ice cream, learns to laugh and to accept life in all its complexities and limitations. Miss Jane comes to understand the practices of the social structure. Her understanding of the dominant society's constraints is best exemplified in her account of the destructive and dehumanizing effects of the system on two brothers, Tee Bob and Timmy, one black and one white. Explaining the injustice inflicted upon Timmy, who is black but whose father is white, by the white overseer Tom Joe, Miss Jane explains:

> He [Tom Joe] hated Timmy with all his might. Timmy got away with too much from that house up there. He knowed that Timmy was Robert Samson's boy, and he hated the Samson in Timmy much as he hated the nigger in him. More, because it was the Samson blood in Timmy that made him so uppity. No, he didn't hit Timmy for what had happened to Tee Bob. He hated Tee Bob much as he hated the rest of the Samsons. He knocked Timmy down because he knowed no white man in his right mind would 'a' said he had done the wrong thing.[17]

Miss Jane understands that on the Samson plantation the working-class whites not only hate the blacks but also dislike the white landed gentry. But the landed gentry will never side with the blacks against the working-class whites, even if the working-class whites are in the wrong: "You pinned medals on a white man when he beat a nigger for drawing back his hand. 'Even a half nigger?' Miss Amma Dean said. 'There ain't no such thing as a half nigger,' Robert said."[18] Miss Jane also understands that this Southern social structure is not only an immense impediment and limitation to the quality of black life, but it also constricts whites' chances of living more meaningful and varied lives. Tee Bob finds himself in a society that does not allow him to love a woman because she is black. The society and its practices have socialized him to believe that black women are at his disposal for sexual exploitation: "If you want her you go to that house and take her. If you want her at that school, make them children go out in the yard and wait. Take her in that ditch if you can't wait to get her home. But she's there for that and nothing else."[19] Rather than rape Mary Agnes, Tee Bob commits suicide: "You don't understand . . . I don't have no place to go." Tee Bob commits suicide because he possesses neither the necessary brutality to rape Mary Agnes nor the courage to defy the age-old Southern tradition.

But most important, the text, through its arrangement of discursive facts, leads the reader to believe that Miss Jane is partly responsible for Tee Bob's death and the deaths of Ned and Jimmy, as well as for the continuation of a brutal and inhumane social system that maims and stifles the individual's mental, emotional, and spiritual growth. The significance of Tee Bob's tragic death is verbalized by Jules Raynard who insists that the responsibility for Tee Bob's death must be shared by everyone, including Miss Jane:

> "We caused one death already this evening," he said. I sat in the back seat looking at him; he was looking out at the rain. "Jimmy was right," he said. "We all killed him. We tried to make him follow a set of rules our people gived us long ago. . . . "
> "I don't understand you, Mr. Raynard," I said.
> " . . . That's why we got rid of him. All us. Me, you, the girl— all us."
> "Wait," I said, "Me?"[20]

In the conversation, Miss Jane understands, as James R. Giles points out, that she and " 'the others' have helped to perpetuate a brutal system by accepting the role of passive 'victim.' "[21] In realizing that passivity contributes to the continuation of this system, Miss Jane comes full circle from being a passive observer to an active, courageous participant who demands change.

In Book IV, *Miss Jane Pittman* repeats its discursive facts and stereotypes. The solitary, heroic Afro-American is represented in Jimmy Aaron, whose individual stand cannot withstand the violence and oppression of the system. The hostile and repressive white ruling force appears here also, as does the passive black community. As in the three previous books, Book IV opens with predictable historical pegs. The time is the early 1960s and Martin Luther King is marching. The civil rights movement is gaining momentum and national attention. Jim Crow practices and segregated laws are being challenged in the courts. The exodus of blacks from the rural South to Southern and Northern urban centers has almost been completed as machinery and technology transform agriculture.

In the midst of these violent, shifting, and ominous forces the text presents Jimmy Aaron. Jimmy, like Big Laura and Ned in Books I and II, becomes the dominant figure. Like Ned, Jimmy recognizes within himself the need to struggle for the salvation of his people: "And it was this, going round with Olivia, listening to people talk, listening to us talk here on the place, what was gnawing in his chest. This was the thing he wanted to let out. No, not out. To let this out he had to both blind himself and defend himself. No, what he wanted was to help. But he didn't know how."[22] To acquire the skills of benevolence, to learn how to serve, Jimmy like Ned goes away to school. Finding himself in a larger social, political, and educational arena where he has greater access to political information, Jimmy like Ned becomes cognizant of the dynamics of the system's operation. He, like Ned, makes decisions as to how he can best assist in its amelioration: through teaching and education. When he returns to Samson, Jimmy brings with him ideas of change, of social and economic equality, and of human dignity. Like Ned he intends to execute social change and to usher in a new social order. But in his solitary attempt to execute certain changes, to bring certain political awarenesses to black people, he, like Big Laura and especially Ned Douglass, is perceived by whites as a threat to their hegemony. Therefore, they murder him.

But in this final repetition of *Miss Jane Pittman*'s discursive facts and stereotypes and their subsequent enunciation, they take on new meanings, and new correlations are established between them. First, there are changes in the discursive passive black community. It has become more sympathetic, receptive, and encouraging to the solitary, daring Afro-American. This change enables a new correlation between the community and the solitary, courageous Afro-American. In the first three books, the heroic Afro-American's move to struggle, to defy the status quo, and to lead emanated from within. His struggle was interpreted by the members of the community as an isolated and unusual incident. Miss Jane goes to the Voodoo Lady about Joe Pittman's dare to break the stallion. Miss Jane and other members of the community view Ned's insistence on teaching the "gospel" as courageous and daring, but they also see it as abberant and as an invitation to death: "And they knowed what he was preaching was go'n get him killed, and them too if they followed."[23]

In Book IV the historical resistance within the black community remains, exemplified by the church members' refusal to listen to Jimmy. But Book IV's discursive black community has a sector, manifested in Jane and others, that merges with the courageous revolutionary force that Big Laura, Joe Pittman, and Ned Douglass represent. Also in Book IV a second correlation is established. In contrast to the previous three books, the text here shows how members of the community nurture rather than isolate "The One" who will lead them to salvation. Speaking about the function of "The One" and his psychological impact on the people, Miss Jane explains:

> Lena was the first one to ask him if he was the One, then we all started wondering if he was the One. That was long long before he had any idea what we wanted out of him. Because, you see, we started wondering about him when he was five or six. . . . Why did we pick him? Well, why do you pick anybody? We picked him because we needed somebody. . . . Jackie and the Dodgers was for the colored people; the Yankees was for the white folks. Like in the Depression, Joe Louis was for the colored. When times get really hard, really tough, He al-

ways send you somebody. In the Depression it was tough on everybody, but twice as hard on the colored people's heart. . . .

Now, after the war He sent us Jackie. The colored soldiers coming back from the war said we could fight together we could play ball together.[24]

The changes within the black community establish a new hierarchy among other discursive facts in the text. As the revolutionary force within the passive black community grows, it undermines the hegemony of the white ruling social order. In addition, the black community's acknowledgment and nurturing of the solitary and heroic Afro-American give him more power and greater influence and significance.

Book IV also presents a change in the discursive fact of the solitary, courageous Afro-American that causes further the establishment of new correlations. Whereas Big Laura, Joe Pittman, and Ned Douglass view their own and black people's salvation as their own solitary mission, Jimmy Aaron knows that the salvation of the people lies within the people. This awareness, which is also fermenting in Miss Jane, is articulated in the speech he delivers before the antagonistic church congregation:

"I don't go to church no more," Jimmy said, "because I lost faith in God. And even now I don't feel worthy standing here before y'all. I don't feel worthy because I'm so weak. And I'm here because you are strong. I need you because my body is not strong enough to stand out there all by myself. . . . Some [people] carry guns, but we know it would be nonsense to even think about that. . . . We have just the strength of our people, our Christian people."[25]

The congregation's response is a clear indication that Jimmy is still ahead of his times. Although Jimmy's mission and Miss Jane's awakening merge in Book IV, it takes Jimmy's death to provoke Miss Jane and the community to act in unity. When Jimmy is murdered, all the forces within the black community that have resisted change are catalyzed. They join Miss Jane in the march in Bayonne.

The shift in emphasis within the text's discursive facts enables

Miss Jane Pittman to reformulate and expand its enunciation. In the American and Afro-American historical past constituted in *Miss Jane Pittman,* the Afro-American historical past is a heroic tradition whose seed is reformulated and replayed during the various epochs from slavery to the 1960s. The repetition of the heroic events and situations within this tradition teaches the black community that individual attempts, no matter how daring and courageous, to defy the dominant society always end in death. Change comes as a result of the masses' determination to act. The individual's defiance functions only as a catalyst to awaken the masses. What the defiant individual fails to realize is that time itself is change, that the individual who attempts to change conditions becomes a slave to history and a stifling social structure, that "people and time bring forth leaders . . . leaders don't bring forth people."[26] The black community learns that change can occur only through group action. *Miss Jane Pittman* ends with Miss Jane, the embodiment of a hundred years of black growth, standing face to face with Robert Samson, the embodiment of a hundred years of white resistance to change. "Me and Robert," she says, "looked at each other there a long time, then I went by him."[27] This confrontation embodies the complete transformation of the discursive facts in the text. The black community that was once passive has become active and in control of its destiny. The solitary, heroic, and defiant Afro-American has become the community. The once hostile, powerful white force has become impotent.

To produce its particular representation of the American and Afro-American historical past, *Miss Jane Pittman*'s discursive formation, which is informed by the sixties' black nationalist discourse, repeats and emphasizes the discursive fact of the courageous, heroic Afro-American who, to maintain his or her integrity and human decency, struggles against enormous odds even if it means death. In giving emphasis to this discursive fact, while subordinating others, *Miss Jane Pittman* dislocates the readers' expectations and sympathies by establishing or manipulating how they respond to characters and situations.

In establishing the enormous odds the solitary, heroic Afro-American must struggle against, the text manipulates the reader into being more sympathetic toward heroic figures than toward certain codified white stereotypes—the terrorist groups or racist white ladies. The text does not give the reader sufficient biographical data to understand the motives behind these stereotypes, to understand why they harbor different responses to the same objects—the Civil War and the Emancipation Proclamation.

Furthermore, the more brutal and oppressive statements among the white population receive more emphasis than those of the more humane whites. In Books I and II, the presence of and emphasis on the Secesh soldiers, Colonel Dye, Albert Cluveau, Tom Joe, and Miss Jane's early mistress, and the consequences of their actions, are given greater textual space than those of the more humane whites such as Robert Samson's wife, Miss Anne Dean, Jules Raynard, or Tee Bob. The oppressive and violent white forces function repeatedly to establish situations where the courage, tenacity, and determination of people like Big Laura, Ned Douglass, and Jimmy Aaron can be displayed. The visibility of the oppressive white forces heightens the Afro-American heroic tradition.

To generate his representation of the historical past, Gaines repeats his strategy of manipulating the reader's sympathies and expectations in Book IV where Jimmy Aaron, the heroic Afro-American, is given a sensitive and "special" portrayal. He is perceived as being intelligent, sagacious, astute, and courageous—all appealing qualities. He writes letters for the elders and he lies to them to uplift their spirits. But the text does not render a similar sensitive and profound portrayal of "that ugly boy of Coon" who reads what is on the printed pages, who is not courageous and daring.

In *Miss Jane Pittman*'s produced representation of the American and Afro-American historical past, we can discern how Gaines produces Other myths and stereotypes, new images, about the Afro-American which counter those produced by Stowe, Twain, Harris, Page, Dunbar, and others. Reverberating against the notion that manhood "is one of the things that the white man has tried to deny the black man ever since he brought him here in chains," the text shows how Joe Pittman dares to die, how Ned conquers the fear of death, and how Jimmy drives home the importance of Joe's and Ned's courageous endeavors.[28] The text produces Joe, Ned, and Jimmy in reaction to the dominant society's denial or exclusion of black manhood in the Afro-American historical past.

Also, in reverberating against the "mammy or . . . nigger wench" image of the black women in the fiction of American writers, *Miss Jane Pittman* produces in Miss Jane another image of the black woman—an image that violates those established by American writers such as Twain (Roxy in *Pudd'nhead Wilson*), Gertrude Stein (Rose in *Melanctha*), Faulkner (Dilsey in *The Sound and the Fury*), and others. In addition to her many roles as wife, foster mother, worker, and friend, Miss Jane is also a distinctly political woman.[29]

Miss Jane Pittman's representation of the American and Afro-American historical past shows how Afro-Americans from each historical epoch have passed on the heroic tradition from one generation to another. Big Laura symbolizes the original black mother, the rebirth of the fighting tradition; and the legacy of her courage, determination, stamina, and unselfish love for Jane, Ned, and black people in general is passed, through the flint and iron, to Miss Jane. This representation also shows how the young rebel against the old and how this rebellion is a necessary prerequisite for change. It is the youth who initiate the changes after the Emancipation Proclamation by breaking down cotton stalks and changing their names. It is the youthful and heroic Ned and Jimmy who break with the hegemony of the dominant society in an attempt to ameliorate the conditions of blacks. Their youthful defiant acts make possible the mass defiance of the 1960s.

This representation also shows how change from within comes from exposure without. Ned leaves the South, acquires an education, does a stint in the army, and returns to the South to preach the social gospel of change. Likewise, Jimmy Aaron—like Grange Copeland in Alice Walker's *The Third Life of Grange Copeland,* like Meridian Hill in Walker's *Meridian,* like Janie Starks in Zora Neale Hurston's *Their Eyes Were Watching God* (who returns to tell other women in her community about her experience), and like Frederick Douglass, Martin Luther King, and Mary McLeod Bethune in the historical reality—leaves his immediate environment, acquires an education, and returns to spread the "truth" to the people. This expatriation, this codified constant that exists in different historical eras, becomes a macrosign in Afro-American literature.

But in illuminating certain facts from the American and Afro-American historical past, *The Autobiography of Miss Jane Pittman* subordinates or excludes others. To show the "heroic deeds" of the Afro-American historical past, the text has to subordinate those facts from the historical past where blacks did not take bold and courageous stands. Walker's *The Third Life of Grange Copeland,* which represents the same historical past, shows Afro-Americans who are passive not only during transitional periods in history but also during their interims. Brownfield, Josie, Mem, and Lorene are passive because they do not possess the tenacity, integrity, and understanding to rebel against the prevailing social structure. Underscoring the theme of the passive Afro-American would undermine *Miss Jane Pittman*'s discursive formation, which argues for an aggressive and progressive Afro-American historical past. Weak men and women do not change history or shape the future; they fall victim to history without any grand consequence.

Miss Jane Pittman's discursive formation excludes the destinies of those Afro-Americans from the historical past who, rather than die in the struggle for "manhood," chose other options—such as singing the blues, playing a musical instrument, becoming a minister, a deacon in the church, or a drunkard or a wife beater. Luzana Cholly and Stagolee Dupas in Albert Murray's *Train Whistle Guitar,* which represents the same historical past, are able to define their existence within the blues-idiom paradigm.[30] This blues-idiom paradigm gives their lives sustenance beyond the oppressive forces of the dominant society. Rather than defy the system, Alice Walker's character Brownfield Copeland vents his anger and frustration on his wife and children.

Miss Jane Pittman's discursive formation also excludes those Afro-Americans from the historical past who are shrewd and cunning enough to violate the norms and social codes of the ruling social order and still live. Uncle Jules of Chesnutt's *The Conjure Woman,* a partial reconstruction of the same historical past, is out to win. Therefore he uses the wisdom of Afro-American culture and folklore to outwit, outmaneuver, and out-scheme members of the dominant American society.

Finally, *Miss Jane Pittman* subordinates the destinies of those black women from the historical past who did not have the courage to take action, who chose options other than being at the forefront of black people's salvation. Some chose to become "failed" or "good time" ladies as in the cases of Josie and Lorene in Walker's *The Third Life.* Others, unable mentally to withstand oppression, committed suicide, as in the case of Margaret Brownfield (also in *The Third Life*).

In identifying the silent and omitted facts from the Afro-American historical past in *Miss Jane Pittman*, we can see how the sixties' black nationalist discourse is one discourse that informs the discursive formation of *The Autobiography of Miss Jane Pittman.* The text selects certain facts—the courageous and heroic Afro-American who struggles against enormous odds; the oppressive white force that allows the text to bring out the strength and courage of the Afro-American; black unity; and certain codified stereotypes—from the historical past which are essential to black nationalism. Then it establishes a group of relations between these facts and other facts from other discourses where they become *discursive.* The relations between these facts enable *Miss Jane Pittman* to make a particular enunciation or closure.

Other discourses that inform the discursive formation of *Miss Jane Pittman* are the nineteenth-century realistic genre—which has built-in limitations, resolutions, and certain codified ways of viewing the real—and Hemingway's stoicism, the idea of maintaining grace under pressure, which is reproduced in Gaines's Afro-American heroic figures such as Joe Pittman and Ned Douglass.

The Autobiography of Miss Jane Pittman joins the collection of other nationalist texts that reconstruct the American and Afro-American historical past—such as William Melvin Kelley's *A Different Drummer* and Alex Haley's *Roots*—and that stress the same nationalist facts and concepts from the historical past. As a collection, they function to make coherent the yearnings and strivings of Afro-Americans. These nationalist texts give Afro-Americans equilibrium, meaning, and historical continuity. They validate, for some, current actions and deeds—especially for those Afro-Americans who accept black nationalism as a way to explain their lived experiences.

When *Miss Jane Pittman* entered the network of the dominant American literary practices, its critics and reviewers were silent on its nationalist ideological concerns. For example, Jerry Bryant argued in the *Southern Review* and the *Nation* that

> Gaines has that combination of moral—sometimes political—commitment and aesthetic distance that characterizes the classic American writer. . . . He does not level any accusations, reflect any specific ideology, idealize any black revolutionary type. . . . Miss Jane is a master of her people's language, with its sensuous vocabulary and its large story of figures of speech. More than that, she is unsurpassed as a storyteller; her knowledge of her subject and the forms through which that subject can best be articulated seems complete.[31]

Geoffrey Wolff in *Newsweek* compared *Miss Jane Pittman* to earlier texts that had similar assumptions about reality: "In this woman Ernest Gaines has created a legendary figure, a magnificent creature of dignity and genius, a woman equipped to stand [by herself] . . . Gaines's novel brings to mind other great works like 'the Odyssey' for the way his heroine's travels manage to summarize the American history of her voice, for her rare capacity to sort through the mess of years and things to find the one true story in it all."[32] Bryant and Wolff imputed literary merits to *Miss Jane Pittman*, and therefore appropriated it because it reproduces dominant literary conventions and practices. It has, they claimed, "aesthetic distance," and it does not "level any accusations, reflect any specific ideology, idealize any black revolutionary type." It resembles the *Odyssey* in the way its "heroine's travels manage to summarize the American history of her race." In their appropriation both Bryant and Wolff are silent, by definition, on the Other in *Miss Jane Pittman*— especially those elements that violate the dominant literary convention of the Afro-American as being docile and safe. They are silent on any analysis or explanation of those assertive and aggressive images —Joe Pittman, Ned Douglass, and Jimmy Aaron—in the text.

However, when defined and interpreted in the Afro-American nationalist discursive formation, *Miss Jane Pittman* is appropriated differently. These reviewers and critics focus on the heroic concepts and categories stressed in the text. They focus on the Other that is excluded by mainstream reviewers. James R. Giles and Addison Gayle emphasize the text's revision of an Afro-American historical past that has been excluded by the literature of the dominant society. Giles argues, "The sense of history presented . . . is not found in the white West. It is a history revised to give some meaning to slavery and a subsequent suffering."[33] Echoing a similar concern, Gayle writes:

> *The Autobiography of Miss Jane Pittman* is a history rewritten and sifted through the mind of a talented novelist. It has been likened to Faulkner's novel, *The Sound and the Fury*—though such comparison has relevance only in terms of themes. The themes of guilt and redemption, enmity and hatred, of men trapped in old patterns are as much a part of this novel as they are of that of the white Southerner. To these themes, however, Gaines has brought a black sensibility, which transforms them and makes them less important than his major character.[34]

Arthenia Bates Millican's review of *Miss Jane Pittman* in the *CLA Journal* focuses on Miss Jane's heroic deeds, strength, and courage: "And that is why we respect Miss Jane; she is noble like the oak. She talks to her tree, that is, she fixes her mind on an ideal to defy the pragmatic reality of a system which allowed men of lesser metal to excel only in inferiority."[35] In stressing how the text rewrites Afro-American history and focusing on heroic characters and deeds, these reviewers and critics accept the same nationalist discursive formation that informs the text. In imputing to *Miss Jane Pittman* the ideological effects of strength and courage, they interpret the text as a cultural object that reproduces their definition of the American and Afro-American historical past.

Chapter 5. History, the Feminist Discourse, and *The Third Life of Grange Copeland*

Just as the black nationalist discourse informs Gaines's *The Autobiography of Miss Jane Pittman*, the feminist discourse informs Alice Walker's *The Third Life of Grange Copeland*—thereby producing a feminist narrative with the function of inventing what Fredric Jameson calls a "formal resolution" to unsolvable "social contradictions."[1] Written in the midst of the feminist movement, *The Third Life* (1970) works upon and transforms the same raw material, the same American and Afro-American historical past, as Gaines's *Miss Jane Pittman*. In its attempt to show the historical oppression of black women and to further undermine established, one-dimensional, stereotypical American images of the black woman, *The Third Life*'s discursive formation produces a feminist representation of the historical past. In an interview with John O'Brien, discussing the writing of *The Third Life,* Walker explains:

> I am committed to exploring the oppressions, the insanities, the loyalties, and the triumphs of black women. In *The Third Life of Grange Copeland*, ostensibly about a man and his son, it is the women and how they are treated that colors everything. . . . I knew when I started *The Third Life of Grange Copeland* that it would have to cover several generations, and nearly a century of growth and upheaval. It begins around 1900 and ends in the sixties . . . all along I wanted to explore

the relationship between parents and children: specifically between daughters and their fathers . . . and I wanted to learn,
myself, how it happens that the hatred a child can have for a
parent becomes inflexible. *And* I wanted to explore the relationship between men and women, and why women are always
condemned for doing what men do as an expression of their
masculinity. Why are women so easily "tramps" and "traitors"
when men are heroes for engaging in the same activity? Why
do women stand for this?[2]

The idea that "the women and how they are treated . . . colors
everything" becomes the major determining factor in the text's
reconstructed historical past. It selects heterogeneous facts from
the historical past. It determines the group of relations the text
must establish to make its enunciation about the historical oppression of women.

Also, in describing the discursive facts that form within *The
Third Life,* we can discern how the text's discursive formation
reproduces statements and facts different in form and dispersed
in time and makes them relate to the same object or enunciation. In the text's discursive formation, these facts are taken
from their original context, intersected, and juxtaposed in what
Jameson calls the "ideologeme" of the text—the "amphibious
formation, whose essential structural characteristic may be described as its possibility to manifest itself either as a pseudo-
idea—a conceptual or belief system, an abstract value, an opinion or prejudice—or as a protonarrative, a kind of ultimate class
fantasy about the 'collective characters' which are the classes of
opposition."[3] In a novel's "ideologeme" these facts take on new
meanings. M. M. Bakhtin writes: "These heterogeneous stylistic
unities [facts], upon entering the novel, combine to form a structural artistic system, and are subordinated to the higher stylistic
unity of the work as a whole, a unity that cannot be identified
with any single one of the unities subordinated to it."[4] *The Third
Life,* then, becomes a product of Walker's feminist intention, her
unconscious and conscious transformation of facts (stylistic unities) from the American and Afro-American historical past that
combine to form a "structural artistic unity."

The text's title, *The Third Life of Grange Copeland*, signifies that protagonist Grange Copeland has three lives and that "the third" life is the most significant. Grange's first life is dominated by his response to an oppressive, dehumanizing social structure that deprives him of his personhood and causes him to abuse his wife Margaret and to deny parental love and care to his son, Brownfield. Grange's second life concerns his journey to New York where he undergoes transformation in preparation for his third life. Brownfield's first life repeats a life cycle, a set of relations, that is quite similar to his father's. Grange's "third" life concerns his return South, his attempt to exorcise past iniquities, to break the desolate social structure, to interrupt a set of relations, in which he and his son have fallen victim. It shows Grange's uncompromising attempt to create a new social structure, a new set of relations, where his granddaughter Ruth can have more options and opportunities in her life than he or his son.

The opening pages of *The Third Life* are filled with actions, symbols, and conventions. These pages show a father who, for some reason, cannot touch or communicate with his son: "His father almost never spoke to him unless they had company."[5] Several scenes later, Grange's wife, Margaret, is presented as a hard-working, loyal, and submissive wife who works in the fields from sun-up to sun-down, who raises a son and manages a household: "His mother agreed with his [Brownfield's] father whenever possible."[6] Margaret as the hard-working, loyal, and submissive black woman becomes a discursive fact that forms within the text. Margaret's scene is juxtaposed immediately with another scene that repeats Grange's refusal to acknowledge his son's presence: "His father never looked at him [Brownfield] or acknowledged him in any way."[7]

Next, *The Third Life* juxtaposes the scene about the father's refusal to acknowledge his son's existence with the scene where Brownfield is watching his father freeze in the presence of a white man.[8] Here we see a master-servant relation between the plantation owner, who is powerful, and Grange, who is subservient and powerless, being constituted in language. The white man as an ominous force who points out Grange's powerlessness, who turns Grange into "a stone or a robot," and who turns the other black men into "objects" becomes a second discursive fact that forms in the text. Grange as a powerless black male becomes a third discursive fact. Finally, in this first chapter, Brownfield as the abused and neglected child becomes another discursive fact in the text.

The scene where Brownfield witnesses his father being humiliated by the white landowner is followed immediately by a scene where Grange is drinking and using abusive language with his son: "I ought to throw you down the goddam well."[9] Here we see the father-son relation being constituted in a language of violence and domination that reflects the master-servant relation between Grange and the white landowner.

With new and repeated discursive facts, *The Third Life* reveals the life cycle, or the set of relations, that not only embraces and embodies Grange Copeland's first life but also reveals the series of discursive facts and categories, their conditions for existence, their limits, and their correlations that form the immediate materials within the text:

> On Monday, suffering from a hangover and the after effects of a violent quarrel with his wife the night before, Grange was morose, sullen, reserved, deeply in pain under the hot early morning sun. Margaret was tense and hard, exceedingly nervous. Brownfield moved about the house like a mouse. On Tuesday, Grange was merely quiet. His wife and son began to relax. On Wednesday, as the day stretched out and the cotton rows stretched out even longer, Grange muttered and sighed. He sat outside in the night air longer before going to bed; he would speak of moving away, of going North. He might even try to figure out how much he owed the man who owned the fields. The man who drove the truck and who owned the shack they occupied. But these activities depressed him, and he said things on Wednesday nights that made his wife cry. By Thursday, Grange's gloominess reached its peak and he grimaced respectfully, with veiled eyes, at the jokes told by the man who drove the truck. On Thursday nights he stalked the house from room to room and pulled himself up and swung

from the rafters of the porch. . . . By Friday Grange was so stupefied with the work and the sun he wanted nothing but rest
the next two days before it started all over again.

On Saturday afternoon Grange shaved, bathed, put on clean
overalls and a shirt and took the wagon into town to buy gro-
ceries. While he was away his wife washed and straightened
her hair. She dressed up and sat, all shining and pretty, in the
open door, hoping anxiously for visitors who never came. . . .
Late Saturday night Grange would come home lurching drunk,
threatening to kill his wife and Brownfield, stumbling and
shooting off his shotgun. He threatened Margaret and she ran
and hid in the woods with Brownfield huddled at her feet.
Then Grange would roll out the door and into the yard, crying
like a child in big wrenching sobs and rubbing his whole head
in the dirt. He would lie there until Sunday morning, when
the chickens pecked around him, and the dog sniffed at him
and neither his wife nor Brownfield went near him. . . . Steady
on his feet but still ashen by noon, Grange would make his
way across the pasture and through the woods, headlong, like
a blind man, to the Baptist church, where his voice above all
the others was raised in song and prayer. Margaret would be
there too. Brownfield asleep on the bench beside her. Back
home again after church Grange and Margaret would begin a
supper quarrel which launched them into another week just
about like the one before.[10]

Within this life cycle, we can identify all the discursive facts
mentioned earlier. Grange, the black man, finds himself in a
subservient and powerless position with regard to the white man
"who drove the truck and who owned the shack they occupied."
Oppressed and abused by the white man, Grange abuses and
mistreats his wife and son. Margaret is, again, loyal and submissive; and the white man as an oppressive force and Brownfield,
the child who is neglected, are also repeated facts.

With this life cycle, *The Third Life* begins to show the conditions of the existence of these facts, their limits, and their correlations within the text. With Grange and the white landowner, a
master-servant relation is constituted in a language of violence

and domination. Frustrated by his powerless position, Grange turns to violence, drinking, and domination. He establishes with his wife and son relations that have the same violence and domination that characterize his relation with the white landowner. Grange's actions and behaviors become the features of his function within the text's group of relations. The white man's sole function within the text is to signify an oppressive and dehumanizing force. The wife Margaret, who is oppressed indirectly by the white man and the existing social structure and directly by the black man Grange, has limited options within the text's group of relations. She can attend to her son when time allows, remain loyal and submissive to Grange, or commit suicide. With both parents caught up in relations that render them powerless and subservient, Brownfield is neglected. The reproduction of these social relations shows how they are transmitted in and through language.

In the production of Grange's first life through its selection, transformation, and arrangement of facts and categories from the American and Afro-American historical past, *The Third Life* produces a particular ideologeme that is different from those made by dominant American discursive formations: the American social system, whose power is exercised by the white male, crushes and emasculates the black man. It stifles his feelings and emotions and it destroys his dreams, hopes, and chances for a better life. The American social structure turns the black man into a beast, suppressing his human qualities and accenting his animal tendencies. The black man, in turn, reflects his violent relation with his white landowner in his relations with his wife and son. He takes his anger and frustration out, not on the social system or the people who exercise its power, but on the black woman, who, like himself in the master-servant relation, remains loyal and submissive, and on his children. Just as the white man becomes the symbol of his oppression, the black man becomes the symbol of the black woman's oppression. Within the set of relations established in the text, we see images of the black woman—as someone who is battered, abused, scarred psychologically, who is "profound, tragic, mysterious, sacred, and unfathomable"[11]—that undermine and violate the dominant

image of the black woman, to use the words of Mary Helen
Washington, as "the one-dimensional Rock of Gibraltar—strong
of back, long of arm, invincible."[12]

These sets of relations within the text embody the problems
that the text must resolve: How will the historical oppression of
women be ameliorated? How will the evil force that causes that
oppression be obliterated? How will the parental love and care
for the black child be reestablished? The seeming intractability
of the text's problems causes the reader to turn the pages, for
each repetition of discursive facts presupposes a closure, an end-
ing. It is this pressure to finish, to find the solution to the text's
problems, that pushes on the narrative.

The Third Life's "ideologeme," its "conceptual complex," is
where, according to Julia Kristeva, the "knowing rationality
grasps the transformation" of the text's set of relations, its facts,
and allows it to project itself variously in the form of a value
system, or in the form of a protonarrative.[13] The text's
ideologeme is the focal point where heterogeneous facts or "stylistic unities" lose their original contexts and meanings and combine to form a "structural artistic system" as determined by the
text's discursive formation.

To generate its ideologeme, *The Third Life* repeats in various
modes and by various means its discursive facts. They are repeated in Josie's rather traumatic life story. Josie's father is bitter toward the world because it has rendered him powerless.
Consequently, like Grange Copeland, he reproduces his violent
and domineering relation with the world in his family relations.
But in this reproduction, he has the power. He displays his anger
and frustration by inflicting violence and humiliation on the
members of his family. At a party Josie gives to earn his love,
she falls: "It was then and only then that her father rose from his
chair, from the garish cushion of war . . . and, standing over her,
forbade anyone to pick her up. . . . He pressed his foot into her
shoulder and dared them to touch her. . . . 'Let'er be,' growled
her father, 'I hear she can do *tricks* on her back like that.'"[14]
And just as Margaret never intercedes when Grange is abusing
Brownfield, Josie's mother refuses to intercede when her husband violates Josie's person and humiliates her in public. Josie's

"father rode her. . . . Her mother was a meek woman and though she rarely agreed with Josie's father she never argued with him."[15]

The Third Life repeats its discursive facts in the cases of the "overworked deacons" that Grange encounters in New York. They beat "their women to death when they couldn't feed them." The discursive facts are repeated again with Grange's Uncle Buster who beats his wife. Each repetition of the text's discursive facts reinforces the signification of the oppressive ideologeme and reformulates the text's problems.

The second life of Grange Copeland, which is the first life of Brownfield Copeland, finds Grange undergoing transformation in New York. As Grange undergoes transformation, Brownfield falls victim to the same dehumanizing social structure that Grange encounters in his first life, and comes to exhibit the same violence as his father.

In the text's strategy of generating its ideologeme, it repeats its discursive facts in Brownfield's life story. Brownfield lives a relatively happy and sedate life until he marries Mem, Josie's niece, and the two move into the Southern sharecropping system. Once in the system, Brownfield gradually finds himself becoming devastated. Despite the fact that he works from sun-up to sun-down, he becomes deeper in debt. Also, as in the case of Grange, Brownfield is denied his role and responsibility of being a husband to his wife and a father to his children—a role and responsibility that the dominant society has socialized him to believe is his. He sees himself becoming a failure:

> That was the year he first saw his own life was becoming a repetition of his father's. He could not save his children from slavery; they did not even belong to him.
>
> His indebtedness depressed him. Year after year the amount he owed continued to climb. He thought of suicide and never forgot it. . . . He prayed for help, for a caring President, for a listening Jesus. He prayed for a decent job in Mem's arms. . . . He felt himself destined to become no more than overseer, on the white man's plantation, of his own children. . . . That was the year he accused Mem of being unfaithful to him, of being used by white men, his oppressors. . . .[16]

Brownfield, like his father and the other black men in the text, finds himself in the powerless and subservient position in a master-servant relation. Like Grange and the other black men, he reproduces this master-servant relation in his relations with his wife and children. He adopts a false sense of pride where controlling his family becomes his only source of power—even if it means resorting to violence. When Mem defies his authority and purchases a home in town, he lies in wait for the first opportunity to destroy her assertive spirit and to bring her back into his fold:

> He determined at such times to treat her like a nigger and a whore . . . and if she made no complaint, to find her guilty. . . .
> He was expected to raise himself upon air, which was all that was left over after his work for others. Others who were always within their rights to pay him practically nothing for his labor. He was never able to build on it, and was never to have any land of his own. . . .
> His crushed pride, his battered ego, made him drag Mem away from school teaching. Her knowledge reflected badly on a husband who could scarcely read and write. It was his great ignorance that sent her into white homes as a domestic, his need to bring her down to his level! It was his rage at himself, and his life and his world that made him beat her from an imaginary attraction she aroused in other men. . . . His rage could and did blame everything, *everything* on her. And she accepted all his burdens along with her own and dealt with them from her own greater knowledge.[17]

Thus, just as Grange's inability to come to grips with his debased and powerless position in society is a principal factor in Margaret's suicide and Brownfield's misguided life, Brownfield's inability to come to grips with his destituted existence is a principal factor in his murder of Mem and his mistreatment of his three daughters.

As Brownfield acts out the drama of Grange's first life, Grange, in his second life, is undergoing transformation in New York where he encounters experiences that will give him a new and informed perspective on his past and will determine how he shapes his future. In Harlem and other parts of the world, Grange has the opportunity to view blacks from a larger social context. He learns about Africa and he teaches himself the history of the black man in America. The culmination of Grange's education is provoked by an encounter in New York's Central Park. When he helps a pregnant white woman from drowning in a pond of water, he is rebuffed and is called a "nigger," which prompts him to allow her to drown. Echoing Wright's *Native Son* where Bigger Thomas feels free psychologically after accidentally killing white Mary Dalton, *The Third Life* explains,

> Her contempt for him had been the last straw; never again would he care what happened to any of them. She was perhaps the only one of them he would ever sentence to death. He had killed a thousand, ten thousand, a whole country of them in his mind. She was the first, and would probably be the only real one.
>
> The death of the woman was simple murder, he thought, and soul condemning; but in a strange way, a bizarre way, it liberated him. . . . It was the taking of the white woman's life . . . that forced him to want to try to live again.[18]

Allowing the woman to drown, Grange is liberated from his fear of whites, a fear that has caused him to mistreat the women and children in his life. With Grange's realization, *The Third Life* hints at a possible resolution to one of its problems, a possible answer to its question of how will the historical oppression of black women be ameliorated?

To live his "third life," Grange returns South where his situation is now different: he has psychological freedom. The soul-searching, the life experiences outside the South, and the educational exposure have allowed him to define himself outside the dominant American myths, conventions, and stereotypes:

> But soon he realized he could not fight all the whites he met. Nor was he interested in it any longer. Each man would have to free himself, he thought, and the best way he could. For the time being, he would withdraw completely from them, find a sanctuary, make a life that they need not acknowledge,

and be always prepared, with his life, to defend it, to protect it, to keep it from whites, inviolate. . . .

"The white folks hated me and I hated myself until I started hating them in return and loving myself. Then I tried just loving me, and then you, and then *ignoring* them as much as I could. . . ."

His one duty in the world was to prepare Ruth for some great and herculean task, some magnificent and deadly struggle, some harsh and foreboding reality.[19]

Grange's "one duty" is to nurture, through Ruth, his granddaughter, a new and whole black life into existence, and this is done at the expense of killing his own son: "Survival was not everything. *He* had survived. But to survive *whole* was what he wanted for Ruth."[20]

Grange's third life serves as a catalyst for the destruction of a social structure that posits definitions of manhood and responsibility which the black man does not have the opportunity to attain; it also resolves the text's problems. As the transformed discursive fact within the text's discursive formation, Grange causes a new social formation, a new ideologeme, to emerge. Now that Grange has replaced his fear and hatred of white with his love for Ruth, he no longer needs to oppress women and abuse children. Grange's psychological liberation resolves the text's problems.

But in this resolution we see how *The Third Life* constitutes what Fredric Jameson calls a "symbolic act, whereby real social contradictions, insurmountable in their own terms, find a purely formal resolution in the aesthetic realm."[21] The oppressive, violent white male who causes the black male to be subservient and powerless is still unresolved in the social reality. This explains why *The Third Life*—in revolving in the aesthetic realm the historical oppression of black women by killing Brownfield and transforming Grange—has to exclude or distance itself from this real political and social contradiction, the oppressive white force, because it cannot directly and immediately conceptualize it.

In addition to the repetition of its discursive facts, *The Third Life* uses other strategies to generate its ideologeme. It uses characters to espouse or to articulate certain cultural, ideological, and sociological forms whenever a given detail needs motivation or reinforcement. For example, when *The Third Life* presents Margaret as hard-working, loyal, and submissive, it invests Brownfield with certain sociological and cultural forms that generate this presentation and the text's ideologeme: "He thought his mother was like their dog in some ways. She didn't have a thing to say that did not in some way show her submission to his father."[22] These sociological forms, which are masquerading as Brownfield's thought, have the penetration, psychological insight, and understanding not of a youth but of an adult. On the one hand, this feminist sociological form supports the text's ideologeme. On the other hand it contradicts Brownfield's chronological years and intellectual maturity.

This strategy is repeated again when Brownfield comments on Josie's suffering at the hands of black men: "Josie, Brownfield was sure, had never been young, had never smelled of milk or of flowers, but only of a sweet decay that one might root out only if one took the trouble to expose inch after inch of her to the bright consuming fire of blind adoration and love."[23] This adult Brownfield has been characterized as evil, as void of feelings and emotions, as the symbol of black women's oppression. Yet in the above commentary he suddenly has insightful and sympathetic comments about Josie's difficult plight in life. Though his comments function to reproduce a feminist perspective, they violate the character of Brownfield as conceived in realist terms of a coherent array of actions and remarks.

This strategy of using characters to espouse ideological forms is further exploited in Grange's transformation. To accent the transforming and redeeming qualities of Grange, *The Third Life* allows Ruth to believe that "Grange drank because of his murderous son and because of Josie. Grange and his wife now rarely spoke to each other; the house was often miserable because of their coldness. . . . But Grange's crimes, she [Ruth] believed, were never aimed at any one but himself, and his total triumph over his life's failure was the joy in him that drew her to him."[24] Like Brownfield's, Ruth's analysis possesses an intellectual insight that is from a perspective much more mature than her chronological years and intellectual development. But Ruth's analysis reinforces the text's narrative move to transform Grange to resolve its problems.

As stated earlier, this strategy of using characters to articulate certain ideological forms causes internal dissonance within the texts and contradictions in character development. These ideological forms, when articulated by characters, are inconsistent with the actions and remarks that have come to characterize the characters. Pierre Macherey, in *A Theory of Literary Production,* argues that this dissonance arises from a text's peculiar relation to its discursive formation, that permits certain facts and excludes others. The text's determinate absences twist its various facts into conflict and contradictions.[25]

In addition, *The Third Life* uses certain established conventions—ideological fragments and sixties' ideological jargon that can be appealed to as acceptable justifications—to generate its ideologeme. It reproduces the psychological rationale conceptualized by Frantz Fanon and textualized by Wright to motivate and justify a textual move—Grange's transformation. Killing one's master as the first prerequisite for the oppressed's psychological liberation was an acceptable ideological form in nationalist circles in the sixties. When Mem, with gun in hand, has the upper hand on Brownfield, she says: "And just think of how many times I done got my head beat by you just so you would feel a little bit like a man, Brownfield Copeland. . . . You going to take the blame for every wrong thing you do and stop blaming it on me and Captain Davis and Daphne and Ornette and Ruth."[26] Brownfield responds to Mem's established cultural form with an "authorative" sociological form: "'Mem,' he whined, assuming weakness from her altered face, 'you know how hard it is to be a black man down here. . . . You knows I never wanted to be nothing but a man! Mem, baby, the white folks just don't let nobody *feel* like doing right.'"[27] In reproducing these "knowing" references, these established and authoritative forms, *The Third Life* is able to reinforce or motivate its ideologeme that when the black man is bruised and dehumanized by the dominant social structure, he, in turn, maims and beats his loyal and submissive wife and mistreats his children.

Finally, *The Third Life* enters into further internal dissonance when it asks from Brownfield a particular statement which its discursive formation denies. To generate the text's resolution to its problem of blaming other rather than self, the text invests Grange with a moral speech condemning Brownfield for refusing to become a man: "I figured he could blame a good part of his life on me, I didn't offer him no directions and, he thought, no love. But when he becomes a man himself, with his own opportunity to righten the wrong I done him by being good to his own children, he had a chance to become a real man, a daddy in his own right. . . . But he messed up with his children, his wife and his home, and never yet blamed hisself."[28] But despite the text's insistence, can Brownfield become a man? Within the text's discursive formation, does Brownfield have the "opportunity to righten the wrong"? Can he become self-critical? Except for the short period early in their marriage when Mem teaches Brownfield to read, when is Brownfield exposed to those social institutions—tradition, examples, education, parental guidance—that will teach him to grow and change? What conditions will cause him to change and grow? Are they present in *The Third Life*? In *The Archaeology of Knowledge,* Foucault argues that there are "conditions necessary for the appearance of an object of discourse . . . which means that one cannot speak of anything at any time."[29]

The text's discursive formation never provides the necessary condition for Brownfield to talk of change or of being a man, as it does for Grange. On the one hand, *The Third Life* reproduces an established definition of manhood—taking care of self and family—that becomes the model for measuring the worth and value of the Afro-American male. On the other hand, the text places that definition of manhood in an Afro-American constellation where it has no chance to materialize. The text even admits that there are no chances: "He [Brownfield] was never able to do more than exist on air."

Yet in Grange's moralizing speech, the text insists that Brownfield is responsible for his own demise. Grange changes because he removes himself from the existing oppressive situation. Unlike Grange, Brownfield never has the option of viewing his debased existence outside the rhetoric of the existing social structure. The only life he knows is the life of the brutal sharecropping system and the language of oppression with which his life represents "reality." Nor does Brownfield, like Grange, have anyone to touch him with love. This internal conflict, again, arises from the text's relation to its discursive formation. The text cannot talk about statements and concepts which its discursive formation denies.

The discursive strategies of including certain facts and excluding others, of arranging these facts hierarchically, of manipulating characters to articulate certain ideological forms—that generate the text's ideologeme—allow *The Third Life* to produce a particular representation of the American and Afro-American historical past from the turn of the century to the late 1960s. *The Third Life*'s produced representation of the historical past makes it possible for it to show the structure and operation of the Southern sharecropping system: certain values, ideas, and feelings that dominated and perpetuated the operation of that system. It also makes it possible for *The Third Life* to show how and why black men made certain decisions about their lives, exhibited certain behaviors, and committed certain violent acts.

In this representation of the historical past, black men— Grange, Brownfield, Josie's father and his friends, Uncle Buster, and the "overworked deacons"—are socialized to believe that being a man means taking control and being responsible for the members of their families. Yet the nature of the dominant society's social structure denies them those controls and responsibilities. This disparity between expectation and actuality causes these black men to develop feelings of inadequacy. Bruised and beaten by the system, they beat their wives and deny guidance and love to their children. In short, they reproduce their relation with the system in their relations with their families.

This reproduced American and Afro-American historical past allows *The Third Life* to show the limited range in which black women have control over their lives and how this limitation makes them dependent upon and loyal to black men. Black women—Margaret, Uncle Buster's wife and the wives of Josie's father's friends and the deacons, Josie, Lorene, and Josie's mother—lose respect for themselves and their husbands and fail, at times, to provide the necessary care and love for their children.

The Third Life shows how the actions of the men "color" everything about the women's lives. After being brutalized by Grange and the sharecropping system, Margaret changes from an earthy, caring, and strong woman to an obtuse street walker. Seeing her own life and her family destroyed by forces she does not understand, Margaret resigns herself to death. Trudier Harris argues that "Margaret's murder and suicide are not defiance; they are a bow of defeat, a resignation to the forces outside. She is *destroyed* by the forces that have dissolved her family."[30] Margaret's inability to find a coping mechanism to give her life order and meaning makes suicide an inevitable choice.

Josie's life is also "colored" by the actions of the men in her life. But despite the fact that she is constantly abused, misused, and abandoned, Josie is still able to care, to exhibit human qualities. After Brownfield kills her niece, she still visits him in prison; and even after Grange abandons her for Ruth, she still defends his honor to Brownfield. She is able still to "love in spite of all that had gone wrong in her life."

Perhaps it is the spectacle of Mem's transformation from a shy, plump, quiet, and intellectual young woman to a skinny, ugly, mentally scarred, and physically maimed woman that allows readers to begin to comprehend the devastating effects of the Southern sharecropping system and of the black man on the black woman. After marrying Brownfield, Mem is dragged from one sharecropper's cabin to another. Her education threatens him; therefore, he embarrasses her in public. When Mem expresses a desire for a house and a better life for their children, Brownfield threatens her with physical violence. Because she spends most of her life struggling to survive amid verbal and physical abuse, Mem never has the time or the option to develop those scholarly, creative, and spiritual interests she had begun to pursue as an adolescent. She is caught in a social web without an exit: "She wanted to leave him, but there was no place to go. She had no one but Josie and Josie despised her. She wrote to her father, whom she had never seen, and he never bothered to answer the letter. From a plump woman she became skinny. . . ."

Even her wonderful breasts dried up and shrank; her hair fell out and the only good thing he could say for her was that she kept herself clean."[31] In spite of Brownfield's abuses, however, Mem still possesses dignity and human warmth. She, like Margaret, continues to work hard to care for and love her family, and she does not become bitter or antisocial. After observing how Mem handles her rather unpleasant predicament with Brownfield, Grange refers to her as a "saint."

It is these "Other" images of the black woman—captured in Josie, Margaret, Mem, Lorene—in *The Third Life* that burst asunder or violate dominant, one-dimensional images of the black woman like mammy, the tragic mulatto, the wench, and the matriarch. This representation of the American and Afro-American historical past also makes it possible for *The Third Life* to show how, when children are neglected and denied parental love and guidance, they can come to hate their parents. After Grange and Margaret have abandoned Brownfield, he cannot forgive them for forgetting that they "were not alone." With no guidance from his mother and father, Brownfield is left to take care of himself, to learn and survive as best he can. Therefore it comes as no surprise that when he marries and moves into the sharecropping system his life begins to resemble his father's. His hopes, dreams, expectations, and person are destroyed. Having never been loved by his parents, he is incapable of loving his daughters. Thus Brownfield passes on to his daughters the brutal kind of human relations that he has learned from Grange and Margaret and their surroundings. This reconstructed American and Afro-American historical shows how social systems and structures are reproduced through language, and how this brutal kind of relationship is passed from one generation to another.

In describing the facts which form within the text, we can see how *The Third Life*'s discursive formation reproduces heterogeneous statements and facts—feminist definitions of history, sixties' sociological jargon, images of black women from other texts, significations of the frustrated, angry, and violent black male from the Afro-American historical past, Fanon's resolution for the liberation of the oppressed class—different in forms and dispersed in time and make them relate to the same object or ideologeme. Brutal and violent facts of the American and Afro-American historical past are related to feminist definitions of history only because the text's rules of formation produce the conditions. The fact of the white male as an insensitive, dehumanizing force is related to the fact of the black woman as being hard-working, loyal, and submissive only because the text's discursive formation needs both to make its enunciation. Sixties sociological jargons are related to the fact of the mistreated and misguided child because *The Third Life*'s rules of formation enable them to form as objects of a discourse. But for *The Third Life* to show certain insights into its produced American and Afro-American historical past and the black life it produces, it has to delimit certain facts and it has to be silent on others.

The Third Life is silent on the many historical moments where black men and black women, despite the oppressive nature of the sharecropping system, have been able to love each other and to occupy the same mental space. These moments exist early in the marriage of Brownfield and Mem before they move into the sharecropping system or before they become adults. These moments also exist between the youthful Quincy and Helen and the old Grange and the young Ruth. But they do not exist during adult life, according to this novel. In comments made to David Bradley in the *New York Times Magazine,* Walker shows how her personal experiences inform her reconstruction of the historical past: "I knew both my grandfathers, and they were just doting, indulgent, sweet old men. I just loved them both and they were crazy about me. However, as young men, middle-aged men, they were . . . brutal. One grandfather knocked my grandmother out of a window. He beat one of his children so severely that the child had epilepsy. Just a horrible, horrible man. But when I knew him, he was a sensitive wonderful man."[32]

In other discursive formations, which deal with the same historical period, black men and black women occupy the same space together. In Gaines's *The Autobiography of Miss Jane Pittman*, Jane Pittman and Joe Pittman are able to draw on the wisdom of the culture and their own inner strengths and determinations to protect themselves from the brutality of the dehumanizing system. Jane—unlike Margaret, Josie, and even Mem — understands the operations of the social system. Therefore she is able to accept its limitations and to live and love within its boundaries. But *The Third Life* cannot talk about black men and black women occupying the same space. To do so would undermine its ideologeme, its conceptual system, premised on the idea that the system's violent treatment of black men and their subsequent violent responses makes that togetherness impossible.

The Third Life is silent on the thousands of black women from the Afro-American historical past who refused to be loyal and submissive to black men, who refused to accept daily abuse from black men. Janie Starks of Hurston's *Their Eyes Were Watching God*, a reconstruction of the same or a similar American and Afro-American historical past, was certainly more aggressive and more independent in spirit and body. Realizing that her first and second husbands practiced values and held ideas that were adverse to hers, Janie leaves both. But *The Third Life* must be silent on rebellious black women, for they represent a category which its discursive formation denies. The presence of a rebellious black woman in the text would counter one of its principle enunciations: that despite the brutality inflicted on them by black men, black women remain loyal and submissive.

Also in *The Third Life*, passive black women produce a sympathetic response from the reader. In denying the reader the chance to witness an aggressive woman's response to this male oppression, *The Third Life* manipulates the reader by having him or her identify with specific characters and situations. The presence of the category of passive black women solicits a sympathetic response from the reader because the reader always identifies with the helpless victim. It also generates the "saintly" image of the black woman. The absence of other options within the text's discursive formation for black men to relieve their frustration and aggressions makes their crimes more brutal and cruel. The reader always has contempt for the violent, aggressive character.

The Third Life is completely silent on other alternatives from the Afro-American historical past that black men historically used to neutralize the brutality of a racist and dehumanizing system. Thousands of black men maintained their humanity, their integrity, and their sanity by turning honestly and genuinely to the church and Christianity. Other black men openly and vehemently defied the system, even at the expense of their lives. An example is Marcus Payne of Gaines's *Of Love and Dust,* also a reconstruction of the same American and Afro-American historical past, who refuses to accept the constrictions of the system. He strikes out against it and meets his death. Likewise Ned Douglass and Jimmy Aaron of Gaines's *Miss Jane Pittman* meet their deaths because they refuse to accept the system's definition of who they are. The presence of discursive facts such as Marcus, Ned, and Jimmy within *The Third Life*'s discursive formation would, again, counter the text's enunciation of the idea that the black man fears the white man and other menacing forces and that, as a result of this fear, he becomes passive.

In making visible *The Third Life*'s discursive strategies and its silences, we can see how the feminist discourse informs *The Third Life*. The text takes hold of certain heterogeneous facts— the domineering patriarch, the violent and oppressive male, the battered, abused mother and child—that are essential to feminist ideology. Then it establishes a group of relations between these facts which enable it to make a particular enunciation, to formulate a particular feminist ideologeme.

The Third Life—along with other feminist texts such as Shange's *For Colored Girls,* Gayl Jones's *Corregidora* and *Eva's Man,* Toni Morrison's *The Bluest Eye* and *Sula,* which reconstruct and emphasize the same American and Afro-American facts and categories as *The Third Life*—gives meaning, coherence, validity, and a history to the strivings and yearnings of a contemporary feminist set of assumptions about women's reality and existence. But, more important, we see how *The Third Life* and other feminist texts are "socially symbolic acts" that invent imaginary or formal solutions to the unresolvable social contradictions. These texts function as indices and cultural messages for Americans and Afro-Americans who embrace feminist ideologies because they explain certain lived experiences. With *The Third Life*, Alice Walker produces new myths about the American and Afro-American historical past—and especially about black women—to counter past and existing myths that have not portrayed women, and particularly black women, as complex human beings who have existed in oppressive and sexist historical constellations. In using the feminist discourse to explain black women's unique brand of historical oppression, Walker also helps that feminist discourse to acquire validity among black women.

Chapter 6. History,
the Blues Idiom Style,
and *Train Whistle Guitar*

The blues idiom style is a definition of existence that is produced by Afro-Americans' historical conditions in America. Barred from full participation in the dominant society's political, economical, and cultural institutions and violated by the subsequent racial oppression, Afro-Americans produced a blues life style and a blues musical form that captured the pain, joy, suffering, irony, and humiliation of their lived experiences. Discussing how the blues style expresses Afro-American life, Albert Murray writes:

> The blues idiom style is entirely consistent with the folklore and wisdom underlying the rugged endurance of the black American. . . . Blues idiom dance music challenges and affirms his personal equilibrium, sustains his humanity, and enables him to maintain his highest aspirations in spite of the fact that human existence is so often mostly a lowdown dirty shame. . . .
>
> The blues ballad is a good example of what the blues are about. Almost always relating a story of frustration, it could hardly be described as a device for avoiding the unpleasant facts of Negro life in America. On the contrary, it is a very specific and highly effective vehicle, the obvious purpose of which is to make Negroes acknowledge the essentially tenuous nature of all human existence. . . .

> The sense of well being that always goes with swinging the
> blues is generated . . . not by obscuring or denying the exis-
> tence of the ugly dimensions of human nature, circumstances,
> and conduct, but rather through the full, sharp and inescapa-
> ble awareness of them . . . to make human existence meaning-
> ful. . . . When the Negro musician or dancer swings the blues,
> he is fulfilling the same fundamental existential requirement
> that determines the mission of the poet. . . . He is confronting,
> acknowledging, and contending with the infernal absurdities
> and ever-impending frustrations inherent in the nature of
> all existence by *playing with the possibilities* that are also
> there.[1]

Because the blues idiom style deals with the "essentially tenuous
nature of all human existence," "the infernal absurdities and the
ever-impending frustrations inherent in the nature of all existence," and "the unpleasant facts of Negro life in America"—
aspects of the human existence that James Baldwin says Americans deny—it is defined as the Other by the institutions within
the dominant American ideological apparatus and is, therefore,
excluded.

In *Train Whistle Guitar* (1974), Albert Murray uses the blues
idiom style and its image of the Afro-American to burst asunder
or violate the dominant American image of the Afro-American
as a pathological, docile victim. Murray argues that this pathological image of the Afro-American is produced by historians,
writers, spokesmen, theorists, and social welfare technicians
"whose statistics-oriented interpretations of black life experience
add up to what functions as a folklore of white supremacy and a
fakelore of black pathology."[2] Murray also sees this pathological
image reproduced in Afro-American protest fiction. Writing in
The Hero and the Blues, Murray argues emphatically against the
"social science-oriented melodrama" (protest fiction) that passes
itself off as literature:

> American protest fiction . . . is essentially anti-adventure and,
> in effect, non-heroic. . . . It concerns itself not with the ironies
> and ambiguities of self-improvement and self-extension, not
> with the evaluation of the individual as protagonist, but rather

with representing a world of collective victims whose survival and betterment depend not upon self-determination but upon a change of heart in their antagonists, who thereupon will cease being villians and become patrons of social welfare. . . .[3]

While the image of the Afro-American as a pathological victim allows the dominant society to integrate the Afro-American into its "natural" order of things, the blues idiom style, as an Other, produces a blues image of the Afro-American that is affirmative, existential, vibrant, and different from the psychological conventions of the dominant society. For Murray, *Train Whistle Guitar* is a counterstatement; it functions to make an

affirmative rebuttal to negative allegations and conclusions about some aspects of Negro life in the United States. . . . since the negative aspects of the black experience are constantly being overpublicized, justice to U.S. Negroes . . . is best served by suggesting some of the affirmative implications of their history and culture. After all, someone must at least begin to try to do justice to what U.S. Negroes *like* about being black and to what they like about being Americans. . . . though images of black masculinity may simply be invisible to Moynihan, it does not follow that they are also nonexistent for Negroes. Thus, while white supremacists were responding to Uncle Toms, Old Black Joe, and Steppin' Fetchits, Negroes were celebrating John Henry, Stagolee, Jack Johnson, and Joe Louis.[4]

Thus, like Gaines in *Miss Jane Pittman*, Murray in *Train Whistle Guitar* intends to reproduce the excluded Other—"some of the affirmative implications" and "images of black masculinity" — from the Afro-American historical past.

But Murray defines *Train Whistle Guitar* as more than just a counterstatement to the various "negative," established American and Afro-American statements about black life; it is also an attempt to define the "universal" in Afro-American life. He wants to "provide a *basis for action* which is compatible with those facts that in instances when Negroes are not involved are generally assumed to represent the universal element in all

human nature."[5] However, Murray's uncritical acceptance of certain "universal" literary assumptions, "the universal element in
all human nature" prevents him from showing in *Train Whistle
Guitar* how Afro-Americans prepare to live in the world with all
its diversity, possibility, ambiguity, irony, and absurdity.
Murray's blind acceptance of certain dominant literary conventions prevents *Train Whistle Guitar* from answering its own
question, and causes dissonance in the narrator.

The title, *Train Whistle Guitar*, conjures up immediately a
blues image. There is the guitar producing and imitating an unusual and transcended sound—a train whistle. The title, as John
Wideman points out, "refers to the capacity of a blues guitar to
imitate and recreate particular sounds . . . reproducing the
rhythm and pitch of the human voice."[6] The title also signifies
the structure of the text: a blues guitar symbolically and literally
re-creating in variations of the blues idiom style the life of Gasoline Point.

Train Whistle Guitar opens with the narrator, in a reminiscent
and "objective" tone, recounting the various locations he had
used to observe life while growing up in Gasoline Point—which
was "more of a location in time than an intersection on a map."[7]
As with Morrison's narrative voice in *Sula,* Miss Jane's narrative
voice in *The Autobiography of Miss Jane Pittman*, and other
texts of the sixties that reconstruct the American and Afro-
American historical past, the narrator in *Train Whistle Guitar* is
returning to and reconstructing an excluded historical past:

> There was a chinaberry tree in the front yard of that house
> in those days, and in early spring the showers outside that
> window always used to become pale green again. Then before
> long there would be chinaberry blossoms. Then it would be
> maytime and then junebugtime and no more school bell morn-
> ings until next September, and when you came out onto the
> front porch and it was fair there were chinaberry shadows on
> the swing and the rocking chair, and chinaberry shade all the
> way from the steps to the gate.
>
> When you climbed up to the best place in the chinaberry
> tree and looked out across Gins Alley during that time of the

year the kite pasture, through which you took the short cut to the post office, would be a meadow of dog fennels again. . . .

The Official name of that place . . . was Gasoline Point, Alabama, because that was what our post office address was, and it was also the name on the L & N timetable and the road map. But once upon a time it was also the briarpatch.[8]

These opening pages present a nostalgic adult narrator who, in recounting his childhood, presents objects or statements that appear ostensibly void of interpretative assessment and judgments: "There was a chinaberry tree," "Then before long there would be chinaberry blossoms," "Then it would be maytime."

The narrator describes Gasoline Point from atop a chinaberry tree. Literally, from this treetop vantage point, the narrator's view is narrow. He cannot see "the post office flag," the switch sidings, the blackberry slopes near the L & N Section Gang Quarters, the waterfront, any part of the downtown Mobile skyline, One Mile Bridge, the pecan orchard, or the African Baptist Hill. Symbolically, this restricted view signifies that unless the narrator has other vantage points from which to observe Gasoline Point, the reader will get a restricted and therefore distorted view of Gasoline Point. In exposing the narrator's restricted view, the text reveals that it is a production, the product of discursive formation.

The second and third brief chapters introduce several discursive facts. In reminiscing about the past, the narrator informs the reader that he has had several names that correspond to several homes: "I used to say My name is also Jack the Rabbit because my home is in the briarpatch, and Little Buddy . . . used to say Me my name is Jack the Rabbit also because my home is also in the also and also of the briarpatch because that is also where I was also bred and also born. And when I also used to say My name is also Jack the Bear he always used to say My home is also nowhere and also anywhere and also everywhere."[9] The "also and the also"—a jazz musical riff that comprises the narrator's past—is captured by the "twelve-bar twelve string guitar riddles" of Luzana Cholly. The guitar captures the narrator's "home." A correlation is established between the music and home. The second chapter equates the blues images of "my home is also nowhere and also anywhere and also everywhere" with the music produced by Luzana Cholly's guitar and the blues idiom life style. The guitar becomes a context for expressing or producing the briarpatch, the life of Gasoline Point: "Because the also and also of all of that was also the also plus also of so many of the twelve-bar twelve-string guitar riddles you got whether in idiomatic iambics or otherwise mostly from Luzana Cholly. . . ."[10] The guitar and the music it produces, which captures the life of Gasoline Point, become discursive facts that form in the text. Home as a blues idiom style that the guitar captures becomes another discursive fact that forms in the text.

Chapter three introduces Little Buddy Marshall and Luzana Cholly. Little Buddy Marshall is associated with blue, which is associated with sunshine, whistling time, and rambling time. He is associated with baseball, which is played in sunny blue afternoons, and Luzana Cholly's blue steel 32–20, and the sound of Luzana Cholly's guitar. Chapter three also introduces the heroic and legendary blues figure of Luzana Cholly. The text makes Luzana Cholly appear larger than life by creating an ambience of mystery: it combines the real with legendary and superhuman qualities: "The more I think about all of that the more I realize that you never could tell which part of what you heard about something he had done had actually happened and which part somebody else had probably made up."[11] In addition to being a "twelve-string guitar player second to none, including Leadbelly," Luzana Cholly does not fear white people:

> the idea of going to jail didn't scare him at all, and the idea of getting lynch-mobbed didn't faze him either. All I can remember him ever saying about that was: If they shoot at me they sure better not miss me they sure better get me that first time. Whitefolks used to say he was a crazy nigger, but what they really meant or should have meant was that he was confusing to them. Because if they knew him well enough to call him crazy they also had to know enough about him to realize that he wasn't foolhardy, or even careless. . . . Somehow or other it was as if they respected him precisely because he didn't seem

to care anything about them one way or the other. They certainly respected the fact that he wasn't going to take any foolishness off of them. . . . He was forever doing something unheard of if not downright outrageous, doing the hell out of it, and not only getting away with whatever it was, but making you like it to boot.[12]

Here we have an Afro-American who rejects the dominant society's language and image and who constitutes himself in a language and a music form that is excluded by the dominant society. Luzana Cholly has traveled extensively, has been to jail, has served time in the penitentiary and on the chain gang, and has experienced unemployment. Although these varied experiences are not sanctioned by the dominant society, they make him an interesting person. They make him a blues person. When Scooter is talking about how he came to know Luzana Cholly, he remembers him "playing blues on his guitar as if he were also an engineer telling tall tales on a train whistle, his left hand doing most of the talking including the laughing and signifying as well as the moaning and crying and even the whining, while his right hand thumped the wheels going somewhere."[13] The left hand symbolizes the frustrations and disappointments of life and the right hand symbolizes the decision to continue with life. Luzana Cholly is a legendary and heroic blues figure whose life is fraught with frustration and personal troubles, and who defines himself outside the dominant society's acceptable conventions and stereotypes. He becomes a discursive fact that forms in the text.

The legendary Luzana Cholly reminds the reminiscent narrator of other legendary blues heroes, such as Stagolee and Jack Johnson, who are also blues heroes and who provided him and little Buddy Marshall with models and examples of human life. The next episode, which is about Jack Johnson, is a derivative of the same blues idiom style:

Because the also and the also of Luzana Cholly (which was also to become at least in part the also and also of Stagolee Kid the piano player) was also the also and also of Jack Johnson who was by all accounts and all odds the nimblest footed quickest witted Jack of them all; who could spring six feet backwards and out of punching range from a standstill, who could salivate a Spanish fighting bull with a six-inch upper-cut, whose eyes and hands were so sharp that he could reach out and snatch flies from mid-air without crushing them.[14]

In this episode Scooter's name changes from "Jack the Rabbit and Jack the Bear," in reference to the briarpatch and the blues sound of Luzana Cholly's guitar, to "Jack the Nimble and Jack the Quick" in reference to the quickness of Jack Johnson. Just as Scooter imitated the walk, the talk, and the style of Luzana Cholly, in this episode he adopts the quickness of Jack Johnson. Scooter has his "cement sack punching bag hanging heavy weight high from the lowest branch of the chinaberry tree. . . . I was not as black or as big as Jack Johnson and I was never going to have all of my hair shaved off, but all the same as soon as I stepped into the prize ring I was the one who had set out from Galveston, Texas, not only to see the sights of the nation and seek my fortune wherever the chances were, but also to become the undisputed champion of the world."[15]

In setting up his "punching bag" and in imagining himself in Jack Johnson's life, Scooter adopts Jack Johnson as a new identity. The qualities that Scooter admires in Jack Johnson are similar to those he admires in Luzana Cholly. Jack Johnson, like Luzana Cholly, has superhuman qualities. He "could spring six feet backwards and out of punching range from a standstill" and he has eyes and hands "so sharp that he would reach out and snatch flies from mid-air without crushing them." Jack Johnson, like Luzana Cholly, lives his life as he pleases; he has scandals in New York and San Francisco. His life is also fraught with frustration and person troubles. He "had to trade his world championship in for his American citizenship," and had to pay "thirty thousand dollars to get back in the U.S.A." Jack Johnson repeats the discursive fact of the legendary and heroic blues figure who lives despite his frustrations and personal troubles. From the way the songs, music, home, and the legendary blues figure constitute themselves in a blues language, and from the "reality" that language produces, we can see how the blues idiom style becomes the text's dominant theme; we can see how the text's discursive facts establish correlations to produce this blues idiom style. The musicians whose lives reflect the blues come from blues communities. The music they play and the songs they sing tell the life stories of their blues communities.

To generate this blues theme about Gasoline Point and the Afro-American historical past, *Train Whistle Guitar* repeats and reformulates its blues idiom style throughout. It is repeated in the episodes of Gus the Gator, Stagolee, and the blues women, and in the male characters in the tales, sermons, and blues songs of the community. In the episode of Gus the Gator, the text again presents Scooter and Little Buddy Marshall with a heroic, superhuman blues figure to emulate as they continue their search for their own identities: "But the only one you needed to be anytime that you wanted to be the Jack Johnson of baseball was the same old long legged sleepy walking Elroy Augustus Gaither better known as Gus the Gator . . . a money ball pitcher" who is so good that he hires himself out during the last innings of the baseball game.[16] Gus the Gator was "supposed to be able to go out in the bottom of the ninth with one run lead and make the first batter pop up to right, left or center; then after waving the outfielders to the sidelines and making the second man hit to first, second, shortstop to third, strike the last batter out with two balls, one called strike plus one of his mess-merizing curves followed by his special of specials the fadeaway."[17] What is admirable about Gus the Gator is "how good he always made you feel, win, lose or draw. Because afterwards everybody always said what everybody always said: Did you see him in there?"[18] It was this quality of style that the people of Gasoline Point found admirable in Gus the Gator.

The discursive fact of the legendary heroic blues figure is repeated with Stagolee Dupas. Stagolee, like all the other principle male characters in the text, overcomes the obstacles that threaten his existence. When Sheriff Earl Joe Timberlake confronts Stagolee, the sheriff's death is the consequence. Also, Stagolee's life experiences—he was "bred and born in the briarpatch"—allow him to know the blues life style and enable him to write blues songs and play them on his "honky-tonk piano."

These legendary blues heroes possess qualities that make them

fantastic and mythic. They are heroic in character and have superhuman qualities. They do not have jobs or power, and their
lives are fraught with frustration and person troubles. Yet they
confront life openly; they deal with it in all its dimensions, possibilities, potentialities, and absurdities. They have mastered the
"irony and absurdity . . . in the briarpatch in which they were
born and bread." They accept and endure life's stress, strain,
and hardship. In assessing the greatness of these heroic blues figures, Scooter explains:

> But then the fact that Luzana Cholly and Stagolee Dupas (fils)
> were road-seasoned gamblers who were almost as notorious for
> being footloose ramblers as for playing music was as impor-
> tant to me and Little Buddy as anything else. Because after all
> if you had been bred and born in the briarpatch, and if like
> me and him you were enroute to Philamayork you had to be
> nimble by habit not only like Jack the Rabbit but also like
> Jack the Bear who could even be nowhere when necessary pre-
> cisely because having been everywhere he knew when you
> were supposed to play drunk or even dead. Anyway, you were
> never supposed to take anything for granted.[19]

In generating further its dominant blues theme, *Train Whistle
Guitar* reproduces the blues idiom style in the community of
Gasoline Point, the briarpatch. Gasoline Point is a community
that has taught itself to confront, acknowledge, and proceed in
spite of, as well as in terms of, "the ugliness and meanness inherent in the human condition." Most members of this community, like the legendary blues figures, are able to sustain their integrity and human dignity even while experiencing personal
tragedy. The individuals who comprise Gasoline Point, as James
Alan McPherson points out, refuse "to see themselves as victims,
refuse to allow their imaginations to become limited by color;
and most important of all, they refuse to concede that human
style and conscious extension of the imagination are not the
most important matters in life. Scooter learns from them."[20]

In refusing to view themselves as victims, the people of Gasoline Point view racial oppression as an obstacle to be surmount-
ed that allows them to learn the best in them, to "make some-

thing" of themselves. They grow to learn the limits of their potentials and the depths of their weaknesses.

In addition, Gasoline Point is a community conscious of the
historical forces that brought it into existence. Never giving in to
others' definitions, this community develops rituals, fireside
nights, legends, and other cultural institutions which function to
pass on its legacies, history, and culture from one generation to
another. These rituals and institutions serve as bulwarks for the
preservation of the race; they counter the dominant society's
myths. For example, members of this community juxtapose their
versions of what happened in the confrontation between the
outlaws—Robert Charles, Railroad Bill, Jack Johnson, Jack
Dempsey—with the white people's versions:

> Mister Doc Donahue was also the one who used to tell
> about how old Robert Charles declared war on the city of New
> Orleans and fought the whole police force all by himself with
> his own special homemade bullets. But the best of all the old-
> so-called outlaws he used to tell about was always the one
> from Alabama named Railroad Bill. Who was so mean when
> somebody crossed him and so tricky that most people believed
> that there was something supernatural about him. He was the
> one that no jail could hold overnight and no bloodhounds
> could track beyond a certain point. Because he worked a mojo
> on them that nobody every heard of before or since. And the
> last time he broke jail, they had the best bloodhounds in the
> whole state there to track him. But the next morning they
> found them all tied together in a fence corner near the edge of
> the swamp. . . .
>
> Naturally the whitefolks claimed they caught him and
> lynched him; but everybody knew better. The whitefolks were
> always claiming something like that. . . .[21]

The people also juxtapose their interpretation of the Constitution, the Declaration of Independence, and the Emancipation
Proclamation with white people's interpretation and practice of
these documents:

> That was also when I used to love to recite the Declaration

of independence, and the Gettysbury Address for them; and I
could also recite the Preamble to the Constitution and part of
the Emancipation Proclamation. . . .

That boy can talk straight out of the dictionary when he
want to, Mister Big Martin said looking at me but talking to
everybody.
It just do you good to hear that kind of talk.
Whitefolks need to hear some talk like that.
The whitefolks they very one said that, Jeff.
What kind of whitefolks talking like that?
Histry-book whitefolks.
Whitefolks in the same book that child reading.
I ain't never heard no whitefolks believing
nothing like that in all my born days.
Whitefolks printed that book, didn't they?
I don't care who printed that book, that's
freedom talk. . . .[22]

This juxtaposition of what the history books say and how white
people interpret and practice what the history books say shows
how interpretation and practice belong to discourse. White people interpret historical documents and the actions of the outlaws
to serve their own discursive interest. But the juxtaposition allows the people to demystify white people's presence and to establish their limitations. It allows the people to defamiliarize the
discourse and expose the strategies white people use to win and
shape consent so that their power, values, and standards appear
both legitimate and natural. In keeping a clear perspective on
their condition and their history, the people of Gasoline Point
are able not only to survive but to live. They use stories about
oppression and other human obstacles to teach the young the
ironies and ambiguities of the human condition: "Sometimes it
would be obvious enough that they were only telling the tallest
tales and the most outrageous lies they could either remember or
fabricate, and sometimes you could be every bit as certain that
their primary purpose was to spell out as precisely as possible
the incontestable facts and most reliable figures involved in the
circumstance under consideration."[23] In showing a community

that is conscious of the social and political forces that not only produced it, but also oppress it, *Train Whistle Guitar* reproduces from the Afro-American historical past an Other community that violates the docile, passive one reproduced by the various institutions in the dominant ideological apparatus.

This reformulation of the blues idiom style in the community of Gasoline Point establishes further the correlation between the category of the legendary and heroic blues hero and the blues community. The blues community nurtures and reinforces the blues life-style not only of its legendary figures but of all its members. This new correlation also reformulates and expands the text's blues theme: that Afro-American life during the period between the turn of the century and the 1960s is blues life. The Afro-American community combined aspects of Christianity, the wisdom distilled from its own historical experiences, the myths and folklores produced by that collective history, to create a social fabric and a worldview that is different from hegemonic American conventions, values, perspectives, and stereotypes.

To generate further its dominant blues theme, *Train Whistle Guitar* repeats its blues idiom style in other modes: Scooter's initiation into the blues life, the sermons and tales, and the lives of the blues women. After Scooter and Little Buddy Marshall have encountered heroic blues figures who have a "somebody-ness," the text's narrator recounts an episode in which he, Scooter, and Little Buddy become adventurous and encounter some of the absurdity of human existence. In the Chickasabogue Swamp, the two experience the randomness of death. They witness the murder of one human being by others without being able to identify a clearly defined motive:

> But that poor sappin somebody back there, he [Buddy] said suddenly. Suppose he was just out there fishing or something.
>
> Man, I said, but bootleggers can tell when you really fishing or hunting.
>
> Yeah but just suppose, he said. Just suppose he was only a stranger and it was night and all he was doing was wandering around lost.[24]

This episode ends with Scooter "still trying to figure out something to say about what he [Buddy] had said. But I was about something else then." This encounter or experience introduces Scooter and Little Buddy Marshall to one of the "infernal absurdities . . . inherent in the nature of all existence."

Just as the repetition of the legendary blues hero generates the dominant blues theme in *Train Whistle Guitar*, the tales and sermons, as blues cultural objects, told by the elders in the barbershops and by the firesides, also reformulate and reinforce its dominant blues idiom style. The tales told by the fireside are replete with heroic blues figures: people who struggle against enormous odds, people whose lives are filled with personal crises. Doc tells the story of Robert Charles who solitarily declared war on the city of New Orleans and successfully fought the whole police force with "homemade" ammunition. There is the tale about Railroad Bill who could work up a "mojo" and break out of anybody's jail. Then there are the stories of people successfully escaping slavery.

The songs mentioned throughout the text reinforce the blues life of the community, and therefore function as cultural objects. Scooter, the narrator, remembers Deljean by the blues song, "How Come You Do Me Like You Do." Women like Miss Blue Ella listen to the blues songs of Bessie Smith, Ma Rainey, and others. The substance of these tales and songs parallels and reinforces the blues idiom style: " . . . and sometimes they [tales] would be telling about some of the same old notorious rounders and roustabouts that the guitar players and the piano players made up songs about."[25] The tales and songs are about surviving frustrated lives, taking risks for freedom, confronting, acknowledging, and contending with the "infernal absurdities" inherent in life, and surmounting obstacles. These cultural objects from the blues idiom style become indices or messages that function to give order, meaning, coherence, and understanding to the lives of the people of Gasoline Point.

One group of individuals who use these cultural objects to give their lives equilibrium is the blues women. On Sundays the blues life manifests itself in church. There is Sister Lucinda Wiggins who

was somebody who was not only trying to go to Heaven whole

soul and body . . . but was indeed over halfway there already. . . . Sometimes she used to become so full of the Holy
Ghost that she used to get up and strut up and down the aisle
from the Amen Corner to the deacon's bench . . . as if she
could walk right on into a pillow of smoke and take the chari-
ot to the Chancery on High. But most of the time it was as if
she was there because it was her sacred duty to see to it that
enough spirit was generated . . . to make somebody else
shout.[26]

After Sunday comes Monday morning when the blues women
display their Monday morning blues. Scooter's mother awoke

saying what I always knew were her prayers and I would know
that she was beginning another week by making thankful acknowledgment to a jealous but ever so merciful Heavenly
Master that it was by His infinite and amazing Grace that
creatures such as we in all our pitiful unworthiness were still
spared to be here to be numbered among the living. . . . the
next thing you heard would be her humming to herself in the
kitchen. . . . That was one way you could tell when she was either somewhat bothered or downright troubled about something.[27]

Just as Scooter's mother woke up humming blues tunes because
she is "bothered" or "troubled about something," Miss Sister
Lucinda Wiggins, across town, is "moaning at the rub board." In
another part of Gasoline Point, Miss Libby Lee Tyler begins
"singing and humming back and forth" with Miss Sister Lucinda
Wiggins. This exchange between the two blues women provokes
the narrator to draw a parallel between their exchange and the
sound produced when "two trumpet players begin trading blues
choruses on an up-tempo dance arrangement, with the trom-
bones and saxophones moaning and shouting in the back-
ground."[28] This parallel further establishes a correlation between
all institutions and practices within Gasoline Point. They reproduce, generate, and reinforce the blues way of thinking existence.
    Within this blues cosmology of Gasoline Point, we are able to
see the success of those blues women and individuals who know

the blues language and who live by the "reality" that blues language constructs. We also see the failure of those individuals who do not. Miss Blue Eula Bocate is successful in living a blues life, while Red Ella is unsuccessful. Miss Blue Eula Bocate has the blues "because she was doomed to be forever childless and in love with a good man who was always gambling his hard-earned wages away."[29] To survive her blues, she begins her Monday morning by winding up her Victrola and playing Bessie Smith. She opens all the doors and windows in her house, removes all the furniture, and scrubs the floors, "plus the porch and the steps." While the house is drying, Miss Blue Eula Bocate continues to listen to Bessie Smith, Ma Rainey, and other blues singers like Mamie Smith, Trixie Smith, and Ida Cox. She works her flowers and sits under the tree. When the house is dry, she returns the furniture to the house and begins her evening dinner. When Mister Mule Bocate arrives home from work, he finds her the same as any other day.

Miss Blue Eula is a successful blues woman because she accepts the blues life, which is reinforced by the songs of Bessie Smith, Ma Rainey, and others. She has her share of frustration and personal troubles, and the blues songs assist her in proceeding with life in spite of the "essentially tenuous nature" of her existence. The blues songs "challenge and affirm" her "personal equilibrium, sustain her humanity," and enable her to maintain high aspirations in spite of the fact that she is fully aware that "human existence is so often mostly a low-down dirty shame." Because she is able to accept and contend with the "ugliness and meanness inherent in the human condition," Miss Blue Eula Bocate is able to survive, to go on living.

However, the successful blues life of Miss Blue Eula Bocate is juxtaposed by the failed blues life of Bea Ella Thornhill, who comes to be known as Miss Red Ella. Bea Ella catches her boyfriend Beau Beau Weaver bedded down with Earlene Barlow and kills him with a knife. As a result, she must "suffer the consequences of murder" and "spend the rest of her life either bent over a sewing machine or floating along in a trance." Her biggest mistake was "not knowing that bad luck and disappointment meant not the end of the world but only that being human you

had to suffer like everybody else from time to time."[30] Bea Ella
fails to understand that pain and suffering are not aberrants but
a part of life, and therefore must be contended with.

The people's response to Red Ella's murder of Beau Beau
Weaver is "I told you so" because their community is

> profoundly conditioned by the twelve-string guitar insinua-
> tions of Luzana Cholly and the honky-tonk piano of Stagolee
> Dupas (fils) as by anything you had ever heard or overheard
> in church at school by the fireside or from any other listening
> post, you knew very well that anything, whether strange or or-
> dinary, happening in Gasoline Point was, in the very nature of
> things, also part and parcel of the same old briarpatch, which
> was the same old blue steel network of endlessly enraging and
> frequently enraging mysteries and riddling ambiguities which
> encompass all the possibilities and determine all the probabili-
> ties in the world. But you also knew something else: no matter
> how accurate your historical data, no matter how impressive
> your statistics, the application of experience to flesh-and-
> blood behavior must always leave something to chance and
> circumstance.[31]

The community of Gasoline Point and its cosmology have made
allowances for the circumstances and events that characterize the
life of Red Ella. These are a part of the "enraging mysteries and
riddling ambiguities which encompass all the possibilities" of its
world. In allowing space for these occurrences, the community
does not overreact, as Bea Eula does, to bad luck and disappointment: "there was neither consternation nor even mild surprise at
what had befallen Beau Beau Weaver. . . . Because although specu-
lation about him may have been prudently vague, it had always
been ominous. It had always included the possibility of violence
because what people had expressed most concern about was not
his integrity . . . but his prospects for simple physical survival."[32]
Bea Ella had been a sweet, innocent, good-looking schoolgirl who
had a propensity for intellectualism. Yet she ends up running
away from her guardian, hiring herself out "as a maid for white
people as if she had never ever been near a school," and giving
her money to Beau Beau to spend on himself.

In the ensuing six to seven months after Bea Ella murders Beau Beau Weaver, the people procure "Stagolee Dupas (fils) to repeat that long since familiar tune at least four or five times every Saturday night." They hope that by making salient the blues tune about what Frankie did to Johnny, they can prevent future mishaps. Thus the blues women generate the text's dominant blues theme that Afro-American life is fraught with frustration and personal troubles, and that it is the blues figure who is able to accept life in all of its possibilities, chances, ironies, ambiguities, and potentialities.

The selection of certain facts and categories from the American and Afro-American historical, folkloric, and mythic past produces a particular myth about that historical past: that in the 1920s the Afro-American had produced a blues language, a cosmology, and a community that reflected their human conditions, their suffering, and an understanding of life that included life's entire spectrum. This community accepts life in all its diversity, possibility, ambiguity, and absurdity. In this acceptance it becomes a part of the same "universal" tradition as existentialism, the Yankee tradition, and the backwoodsman.[33] Like existential reality, this blues community confronts, acknowledges, and contends with "the infernal absurdities and ever impending frustrations inherent in the nature of existence." As a briarpatch, this blues community possesses people from all races. Gasoline Point as a place where people of diverse backgrounds and heritages live is displayed when Scooter tells how he comes to know what Unka Jojo meant when he said that he was an African:

> Anyway it was some time before I was to think any more about Unka Jojo being an African than about Blue Gum Geechee Silas the West Indian handyman or about Jake Hugh or JQ or Jacques Martinet the Creole fish and oyster peddler or about Chastang Cholly the Cajun nightwatchman or Chief Big Duck the Chickasaw Indian or Lil Duck the Choctaw Indian or Miss Queen Minnie Jo-Buck who was suppose to be a Black Creek Indian because she had coal black velvet-smooth skin and jet black glossy hair that came all the way down to her waist.[34]

As a "universal" community, Gasoline Point is equipped to provide its youth with models and examples that will prepare them to survive and live anywhere.

In reproducing the legendary and heroic blues figures, the blues women, the songs, sermons, tales, and the community of Gasoline Point, *Train Whistle Guitar* violates the dominant American stereotype—reproduced in the "social science-oriented melodrama" produced by historians, spokesmen, theorists, and social welfare technicians and in the protest fiction of Richard Wright and others—of the Afro-American as an inferior pathological victim who functions to generate white supremacy in the dominant American ideological apparatus. Instead, *Train Whistle Guitar* presents in the Afro-American historical past an Afro-American, an Other, who defines himself or herself as a blues figure capable of confronting, acknowledging, and contending with the ugliness and meanness in the human condition. It produces an Afro-American who can accept the spectrum of the human existence.

In addition to the repetition and reformulation of the blues idiom style, *Train Whistle Guitar* uses other discursive strategies to generate its blues myth about the American and Afro-American historical past. Its narrator is presented as being astute intellectually on issues and facts that reproduce the text's dominant blues theme. The narrator also is innocent and intellectually naive on discursive facts and issues that counter or undermine its blues theme. This narrative technique causes dissonance and contradiction in the narrator's character development. James Alan McPherson, in his "The View from the Chinaberry Tree," comments that Albert Murray is among "a few black writers" who have to think "consciously about ways in which their history can be made accessible as art. For one thing, they avoid ideology."[35] But the mere fact that *Train Whistle Guitar* permits and excludes certain facts from the Afro-American historical past shows that it is informed by discourse or an ideology. For example, the narrator has no knowledge of the impact of racism on Luzana Cholly's life—the racial significance and ramifications of Luzana Cholly's going to jail or doing time in the penitentiary. (Without understanding these issues, the narrator can perceive

Luzana Cholly as a legendary blues figure who can play his guitar "second to none" and who can stand up to white people.) Yet the narrator has profound intellectual insight into white people's psychology, as well as into blues music and the blues life.

Although the narrator does not have the mature social insight to comprehend or pass judgment on the political reason for Jack Johnson's trading his world championship for his American citizenship, he has sufficient critical skills to analyze the behavior and actions of the Continental Army and General Washington, who "whip slackers and stragglers and would be deserters back into the rank." He is astute enough to know that Washington's action belongs to an American tradition—even when practiced by black Americans: "All of which was what Give me Liberty or give me death really meant, which was why whenever you talked about following in the footsteps of our great American forefathers you were also talking about the bloody tracks the half barefooted troops left in the snow that fateful winter."[36]

The narrator, an obviously astute American constitutionalist, does not ask questions or pass judgments on why Gus the Gator, a money ball pitcher and an extraordinary baseball player, is not playing in the World Series. He does not ask why Gus the Gator leaves "Mobile for Kansas City and points North." Is it institutional racism that prevents him from playing professional baseball? Is it Gus's inability to find stable, viable employment that causes him to move North? For the narrator to ruminate on these questions or to deal with the precariousness of Jack Johnson's and Gus the Gator's futures is to challenge the superhuman images of the blues figures who can produce magic on the baseball field or who can "reach out and snatch flies from mid-air without crushing them." Yet in other instances the narrator seems capable. Why this dissonance in his development?

The dissonance in the narrator's character development lies in the fact that when the narrative voice is mature, insightful, critical, and astute in its commentary or account, it is reinforcing the dominant blues theme in the text. When the narrative voice is silent on other facts, or fails to be equally as insightful and intellectually profound in its treatment of them, it is also reinforcing

the dominant blues theme in the text. As Terry Eagleton points
out in *Criticism and Ideology,* when a text produces the personal
or historical reality, it casts a shadow on its absence over the
perception of its presence.[37] This means that its presence exists
as a result of certain absences.

Conflict in *Train Whistle Guitar* is further generated when the
narrator presents certain characters as blues women without providing sufficient historical or personal data. With the exceptions
of Bea Ella Thornhill, whose man is an infidel, and Miss Eula
Bocate, who is childless and is in love with a good man who
gambles, the text does not provide evidence for women to be
classified as blues women. The reader never comprehends fully
why Scooter's mother, Miss Sister Lucinda Wiggins, Miss Big
Martha Sanford, Miss Honey Houston, and Miss Edwina are
shouting the blues in church every Sunday and crying the blues
at home every Monday morning. The reader is never informed
as to why Scooter's mother arises on Monday morning "humming to herself in the kitchen," or why Miss Libby Lee Tyler begins "singing and humming back" to Miss Sister Lucinda Wiggins.

In producing multiple signifiers of blues women, *Train Whistle
Guitar* dislocates the tendencies of its readers by inundating
them with multiple types of the same character within the Afro-
American historical, folkloric, and mythic past. In the absence of
other types of characters, readers are deluded into believing that
the text really is talking about the Afro-American historical past,
and are manipulated into believing the dominant meaning within the text: that Afro-American life is blues life.

But this dissonance has grave consequences for the polysemic
quality of the text. In producing silences within its narrative
voice, the text stifles the growth and development of the narrator. As the text opens, the reader is presented with a matured
and supposedly sagacious narrator who, in recounting incidents
from his childhood, intends to inform the reader how he grew
and developed as a result of the "universal" experiences and
myriad people he encountered in Gasoline Point. But due to the
text's exclusion of certain facts from the Afro-American historical past, the narrator never informs the reader of this growth
and development.

With the exceptions of the times when Scooter knows that Stagolee will destroy the sheriff and that "bad luck and disappointment" does not mean the end of the world (as in the case of Bea Ella) *Train Whistle Guitar* does not show the development, maturation, and intellectual growth of Scooter, the narrator. Although he emulates Luzana Cholly and listens to a long lecture from him on education, the narrator shows no evidence of growth. Lessons about the history and culture of black Americans are disseminated by the firesides and in the barbershops. Yet the narrator makes no decision, participates in no narrative actions to indicate that he has acquired greater insight into the ambiguities and absurdities of the human condition, that he understands or has internalized any of these lessons.

The reader never witnesses the narrator/protagonist working through and learning from the ironies and ambiguities of human existence, and ultimately reaching the mature stage of an existential or blues hero who has "somebodyness." The reader is further denied the complex process of watching the narrator/protagonist extrapolate, make decisions, endure stress and strain, take risks and chances, and live with the consequences of those chances and risks. In short, the reader never witnesses the narrator developing into a blues hero. But Murray views heroic adventures—whether they are successful or not is irrelevant—as a prerequisite for a good story: "all great storytellers have always known that irony and absurdity are not only thorns in the briarpatch in which they themselves were bred and born but also precisely what literary statement is forever trying to provide adequate terms for."[38]

The question we are forced to ask about *Train Whistle Guitar* is why, as a "literary statement," it does not "provide adequate terms for . . . irony and absurdity" in the narrator. The presence of this "literary statement" in the narrator could show the vastness of the human condition within which the narrator/protagonist must live. Its presence could show the narrator/protagonist's tenuous and vulnerable human position as he chooses to live and make decisions amid the "endlessly engaging and frequently enraging mysteries and riddling ambiguities which encompass all the possibilities and determine all the probabilities in the world."

But in order for the protagonist to take risks and to make decisions he must be able first to think and second to act. Stephen Dedalus in James Joyce's *The Portrait of an Artist as a Young Man* and Roquentin in Jean-Paul Sartre's *Nausea,* both existential or blues heroes, make decisions, take risks, and act. Both confront and deal with political and social forces that act upon their lives. For example, it is Stephen Dedalus's confrontation with Ireland's nationalism and Catholicism and their subsequent repression that lead to his exile. In its attempt to eschew the political and social implications of narrative actions, *Train Whistle Guitar* entraps the narrator/protagonist in dominant American values and conventions that have universalized their ideological base.

First, Albert Murray accepts established literary conventions, stereotypes, perspectives, and definitions that allow him to exclude other literary forms and conventions. When Murray says that "all great storytellers have always known that irony and absurdity are . . . precisely what literary statement is forever trying to provide adequate terms for," he establishes a "universal" standard for determining the worth and value of literary texts. His inability to defamiliarize, to see the ideological function, of this established myth about literature allows him to denounce those literary texts that do not reproduce this literary myth. But, more important, Murray's focus on those "universal" human elements — as they are defined by this ideologically produced literary myth—in Afro-American blues life causes him to exclude social and political implications that underlie that life. For example, the suffering encountered by the characters in *Train Whistle Guitar* is not the result of white people or institutional racial exclusion by the dominant ideological apparatus. Rather, the suffering, bad luck, misfortune, denied opportunity, and disappointment are simply inevitable elements of life. They are not "restrictions of an oppressive political system," but "inscrutable 'Olympian' contradictions and humiliations of human existence itself."

Second, Albert Murray assumes that "great literature" transcends ideology. In *The Omni-Americans,* he comments: "Polemics, however, are not likely to be epics. They are likely to be pamphlets, even when they are disguised as stories and plays. . . . there are many reasons why it is all but impossible for a serious writer of fiction to engage his craft as such in a political cause, no matter how worthy, without violating his very special integrity as an artist in some serious way."[39] We know that ideology is a practice that works on the raw material of social relationships with the instruments of ideological (or discursive) production provided by its subject-centered structure. In *Train Whistle Guitar,* Murray uses the blues idiom style and conventions from the existential literary discourse to work on the raw material of the Afro-American historical past. This means that *Train Whistle Guitar* is as much an ideologically produced text as any black nationalist text, or any text by Richard Wright. The problem is that *Train Whistle Guitar* reproduces more of the dominant literary values and works from many of the dominant literary assumptions, and therefore appears more "natural" and less dominated by ideology than a black nationalist text.

Train Whistle Guitar reproduces dominant literary conventions from Hemingway, Faulkner, Joyce, and others. It reproduces aspects of existentialism and Hemingway's concept of the hero as a figure whose deeds merit status because he confronts and slays dragons. Murray writes:

> Heroism . . . is measured in terms of the stress and strain it can endure and the magnitude and complexity of the obstacles it overcomes. Thus difficulties and vicissitudes which beset the potential hero on all sides not only threaten his existence and jeopardize his prospects; they also, by bringing out the best in him, serve his purpose. They make it possible for him to make something of himself. Such is the nature of every confrontation in the context of heroic action.[40]

The legendary blues heroes, in triumphing over the "difficulties and vicissitudes" that beset them and in enduring the "stress and strain" and the "magnitude and complexity of the obstacles," reproduce Hemingway's concept of heroism. But Murray sees this heroism manifested not only in the fiction of Joyce, Mann,

Hemingway, and Eliot, but also in the Afro-American blues art form: "We learn . . . from Mann, Joyce, Hemingway, Eliot and the rest, but I am also trying to learn to write in terms of the U.S. tradition I grew up in, the tradition of blues, stomps, ragtime, jumps and swing. . . ."[41] *Train Whistle Guitar* also reproduces aspects of the stream-of-consciousness technique practiced by Joyce, Proust, and Faulkner. With this technique, the real is constituted by an association of ideas. The first idea evokes the second, and the occurrence of these ideas associatively in the consciousness constitutes the real. For Murray, the stream-of-consciousness technique has the same repetitive pattern as blues and swing improvisation, which is a variation on the same thematic structure or idea.

The literary tradition and values of Joyce, Mann, Faulkner, and others become the context Murray uses to reproduce the blues idiom style from the Afro-American historical past. In reproducing this tradition and these values, Murray in *Train Whistle Guitar* accepts specific forms of the dominant literary discourse that allow the text to appear "natural" and void of ideology. This reproduction also affects the text's reception by mainstream critics.

But this literary tradition, these values, allow Murray not only to show that the Afro-American blues idiom style has features similar to traditions within the dominant literary discourse and is therefore as "universal" as they are, but also to produce an Other Afro-American historical past that violates the versions produced by the dominant ideological apparatus. Murray's representation of the Afro-American historical past does not show the Afro-American as a pathological victim. It shows him as someone who defines his existence within the blues idiom style, which is capable of dealing with life in all its complexities, possibilities, ambiguities, and absurdities.

Chapter 7. The Song of Morrison's *Sula:*
History, Mythical Thought, and
the Production of the Afro-American
Historical Past

Many literary critics and reviewers are stupefied by the fictive world of Toni Morrison. The values, codes, conventions, and cosmology of her fictive world violate these critics' and reviewers' sense of order, question their bodies of knowledge, disrupt their linear and rational perceptions of time, and challenge their ways of knowing and defining reality. In her interview with Morrison in the *American Rag,* Ntozake Shange avers that there are "things" in Morrison's fiction "that demand we move away from a linear view of the universe."[1] Writing in the *New York Times Magazine,* Colette Dowling surmises: "There is an atmosphere of exoticism, honed at times to the intensity of magic, that gives much of Toni Morrison's work a surreal quality. . . . Morrison gives us exotic stuff—voodoo dolls, greenish-gray love potions. . . . There are natural healing practices. . . . excesses of love and hate that bend the mind and fell the body."[2] Reviewing *Sula,* Diane Johnson, in the *New York Review of Books,* comments: "In *Sula* a mother pours gasoline over her son and lights it, and, in another place, a young woman watches with interest while her mother burns. But the horrors . . . are nearly deprived of their grisliness by the tone. It might be a folktale in which someone cuts someone else's heart out and buries it under a tree, from which a thorn bush springs, and so on."[3] And in his interview with Morrison in *Nimrod,* Pepsi Charles reveals to Morrison that "when I read one of your books I always enter another world."[4] If the three previously discussed Afro-American texts are the products of discursive formations as they produce representations of the American and Afro-American historical past, what are Morrison's intentions in producing *Sula*? How does *Sula* represent that same historical material? What are the rules of formation that produce *Sula*? What are the statements and concepts that inform *Sula*?

In Colette Dowling's "The Song of Toni Morrison," Morrison specifies her concern for a particular cosmology that comprises Afro-America. She says she is concerned with "the elaborately socialized world of black people. . . . I wanted to find out who those people are . . . and why they live the way they do. I want to see the stuff out of which they're made."[5] In Paula Giddings's "The Triumphant Song of Toni Morrison," Morrison delineates further her particular interest in this Afro-American cosmology: "I'm not interested in happiness in my work. I'm interested in survival—who survives and why they survived."[6] From these comments, we can surmise that Morrison, unlike Gaines in *Miss Jane Pittman* and Murray in *Train Whistle Guitar*, will not focus on heroic black figures, "affirmative implications," or the "white oppressor." Unlike Walker in *The Third Life,* Morrison is not concerned directly with the oppressive social and human forces that destroy black life. But like Murray in *Train Whistle Guitar,* Morrison is concerned with that Other Afro-American whose depth and complexity cannot be presented fully by existing ideological and literary labels and categories. Morrison is concerned with the various ways and means by which blacks survived social oppression and natural disasters; she like Murray is concerned with the ontological structures and mythical thought systems, outside those appropriated by the dominant society, that blacks developed to define and reinforce their definitions of self and existence. In short, Morrison in *Sula* is concerned with those Afro-American belief structures, and the "reality" they produce, that emanate from a non-rational Afro-American source: "I am very superstitious. And that is a word that is in disrepute, but whatever it is that I am has nothing to do with my relationship to things other than human beings. In *Sula* the people are like people I have always known who may or may not be superstitious but they look at the world differently. Their cosmology is a little bit different."[7] Therefore one fact, statement, or concept that informs *Sula* and its representation of the Afro-American historical past is magic, the surreal—an element alien to rationalism or the rational society.

A second statement that informs the production of *Sula* is the need, according to Morrison, for blacks to reintroduce themselves to their historical past—a past that has been buried by the emergence of the sixties movement: "Everybody was talking . . . about either slavery or the '60s. And I thought 'There is so much history in between'. . . . We have to know what the past was so that we can use it for now. . . ."[8] In an article entitled "Rediscovering Black History," Morrison explains further her reactions to the sixties, which also inform the production of *Sula*:

> During those intense years [the sixties], one felt both excitement and a sense of loss. In the push toward middle-class respectability, we wanted tongue depressors sticking from every black man's coat pocket and briefcases swinging from every black hand. In the legitimate and necessary drive for better job and housing, we abandoned the past and a lot of the truth and sustenance that went with it. And when Civil Rights became Black Power, we frequently chose exoticism over reality. The old verities that made being black and alive in this country the most dynamite existence imaginable . . . were being driven underground—by blacks. . . . In trying to cure the cancer of slavery and its consequences, some healthy as well as malignant cells were destroyed. . . . For larger and larger numbers of black people, this sense of loss has grown, and the deeper the conviction that something valuable is slipping away from us, the more necessary it has become to find some way to hold on to the useful past without blocking off the possibilities of the future. . . .[9]

Morrison believes that her generation, which was busy striving to become middle-class and to be accepted by the dominant American society, failed to "tell somebody something," failed to pass on certain indispensable "truth and sustenance" to succeeding generations.[10] In *Sula* she reproduces the black neighborhood to show the "useful past . . . our intelligence, our resilience, our skill, our tenacity, irony or spiritual health"—the "stuff" black people have used historically to survive:

> My tendency is to focus on neighborhoods and communities. . . . And there was this life-giving, very, very strong sustenance that people got from the neighborhood. One lives, really, not so much in your house as you do outside of it, within the "compounds," within the village or whatever it is. And legal responsibilities, all the responsibilities that agencies now have, were the responsibilities of the neighborhood. So that people were taken care of, or locked up or whatever. If they were sick, other people took care of them; . . . if they needed something to eat, other people took care of them; if they were mad, other people provided a small space for them, or related to their madness or tried to find out the limits of their madness.
>
> They also meddled in your lives a lot. They felt that you belonged to them. And every woman on the street could raise everybody's child, and tell you exactly what to do and you felt that connection with those people and they felt it with you.[11]

A third force that informs the production of *Sula* and its representation of the historical past is feminism—the emphasis on viewing black women as complex human beings. In a review of *Portraits In Fact and Fiction,* edited by Mel Watkins (during the period when Morrison had published *The Bluest Eye* and was writing *Sula*), Morrison writes: "Somewhere there is, or will be, an in-depth portrait of the black woman. At the moment, it resides outside the pages of this book. She is somewhere, though, some place, just as she always has been, up to her pelvis in myth."[12] There is also Morrison's concern about black women who have always had the kind of friendship traditionally associated with men: "People talk about the friendship of women, and them having respect for each other, like it's something new. But Black women have always had that, they always have been emotional life supports for each other."[13] These feminist concerns inform the production of *Sula* and determine how it represents women in the Afro-American historical past.

A fourth and final concept that informs the production of *Sula* is audience. In response to a question about why she tends to "exclude white people" from her fiction and to "focus on how blacks deal with each other," Morrison retorts: "That's [the focus on blacks] much more important to me than a posture that we may or may not take against 'the oppressor,' or white people who give us jobs or not. . . . What one does with one's own life under the given situation . . . is what is fascinating to me."[14] In identifying the audience to whom she is writing, Morrison asserts emphatically:

> I felt that nobody talked about or wrote about those Black people the way I knew those people to be. And I was aware of that fact, that it *was* rare. Aware that there was an enormous amount of apology going on, even in the best writing. . . . But more important than that, there was so much explanation . . . the black writer always explained something to somebody else. And I didn't want to explain anything to anybody else. . . .
>
> I always wanted to read Black books in which *I* was enlightened, I as a Black person. . . . There are not many books like that. . . . The Black people who never pick up a book—the Black people in *my* books who don't read books—are the people who authenticate that book for me.[15]

Finally, as to why her major characters are unusually exotic by "modern standards," Morrison says, "I write about them not because they are common characters, but because they are uncommon. . . . I don't want to know what happens with somebody who does the routine."[16] Morrison's awareness of a particular audience further informs *Sula's* representation of the Afro-American historical past.

Sula's discursive formation delimits the heterogeneous facts and categories from the historical past that will be specific to its production. It orders these statements and facts, establishes their correlations, assigns them positions, and arranges the hierarchy of their importance within the text's space. Through this delimitation *Sula* produces an Other representation of the Afro-American historical past that is different from those normally sanctioned by the institutions—critics, reviewers, editors, and publishers—within the dominant American ideological apparatus. This representation gives a coherent history to those post-sixties Afro-Americans who define themselves by more than rational, codified categories such as linear time, reason, empiricism, and realism.

Sula, published in 1974 at the peak of the women's movement and at a reflective moment in the black movement, begins as follows:

> In that place, where they tore the nightshade and blackberry patches from their roots to make room for the Medallion City Golf Course, there was once a neighborhood. It stood in the hills above the valley town of Medallion and spread all the way to the river. . . . One road, shaded by beeches, oaks, maples and chestnuts, connected it to the valley. The beeches are gone now, and so are the pear trees where children sat and yelled down through blossoms to passersby. Generous funds have been allotted to level the stripped and faded buildings that clutter the road from Medallion up to the golf course. They are going to raze the Time and a Half Pool Hall, where feet in long tan shoes once pointed down from chair rungs. A steel ball will knock to dust Irene's Palace of Cosmetology, where women used to lean their heads back on sink trays and doze while Irene lathered NuNile into their hair. Men in khaki work clothes will pry loose the slats of Reba's Grill, where the owner cooked in her hat because she couldn't remember the ingredients without it.[17]

This opening paragraph presents numerous statements and raises many questions. The two phrases, "in that place" and "there was once a neighborhood," suggest that *Sula* is about a "place," a "neighborhood" that existed in the past but is now being devastated. This opening paragraph also signifies that the neighborhood has a nonrational or superstitious component—"where the owner cooked in her hat because she couldn't remember the ingredients without it."

The image of the neighborhood's destruction functions stylistically to establish *Sula's* essential question: Why is the neighborhood being replaced by a golf course? As a result, structurally,

Sula poses an enigma, a question, and then teases the reader through the progression of the narrative actions until the enigma is resolved, the question is answered.

The first chapter also gives the reader further insight into the composition of this neighborhood:

> on quiet days people in valley houses could hear singing some-
> times, banjos sometimes, and, if a valley man [white man]
> happened to have business up in those hills . . . he might see a
> dark woman in a flowered dress doing a bit of cakewalk, a bit
> of black bottom, a bit of "messing around" to the lively notes
> of a mouth organ. . . . The black people watching her would
> laugh and rub their knees, and it would be easy for the valley
> man to hear the laughter and not notice the adult pain that
> rested somewhere under the eyelids, somewhere under their
> head rags and soft felt hats, somewhere in the palm of the
> hand, somewhere behind the frayed lapels, somewhere in the
> sinew's curve. He'd have to stand in the back of Greater Saint
> Matthew's and let the tenor's voice dress him in silk, or touch
> the hands of the spoon carvers (who had not worked in eight
> years) and let the fingers that danced on wood kiss his skin.
> Otherwise the pain would escape him even though the laughter
> was part of the pain.[18]

Pervaded with images and symbols of the blues, this chapter reveals the human condition of the neighborhood. It is a condition characterized by unemployment, pain, and suffering that manifest themselves in music, dance, and laughter. The laughter functions to alleviate the pain, to make life bearable.

Subsequent paragraphs of this chapter recount the history of the neighborhood and describe its conception as a "nigger joke." Betrayed by the white farmer who promises him "freedom and a piece of bottom land" if he will assist him with some "difficult chores," the slave, powerless to demand retribution, takes the "bottom land" in the hills. The first chapter ends with the valley people developing myths about what was happening "up in the Bottom." But, the black people had other things in mind. They "were mightily preoccupied with earthly things—and each other, wondering even as early as 1920 what Shadrack was all about,

what that little girl in *Sula* who grew into a woman in their town
was all about, and what they themselves were all about, tucked
up there in the Bottom."[19] The significance of this final com-
ment is twofold. It indicates the focus of *Sula*—on the "people
up in the Bottom," especially Shadrack and Sula, the inner tis-
sues of their lives, and their cosmology. Second, it relocates the
reader to a particular historical moment, the 1920s, in the
American and Afro-American historical past.

Chapter two—"1919"—introduces Shadrack who is "blasted
and permanently astonished by the events of 1917." Mentally
deranged by his participation in World War I, Shadrack is released from the hospital because it needs his space. Shadrack
finds himself forlorn and destitute: "Twenty-two-years old, weak,
hot, frightened, not daring to acknowledge the fact that he didn't
even know who or what he was . . . with no past, no language, no
tribe, no source, no address book, no comb, no pencil, no clock
. . . no bed . . . and nothing to do."[20] He is arrested and is later
released to a farmer who returns him to Medallion.

It is in Medallion that Shadrack devises a scheme and establishes a bulwark to protect his vulnerabilities and human frailties. He struggles to sort out his relation to fear and death and to
define a framework that will give his life order or equilibrium.

> [It was] a struggle that was to last for twelve days, a struggle to
> order and focus experience. It had to do with making a place
> for fear as a way of controlling it. He knew the smell of death
> and was terrified of it, for he could not anticipate it. It was
> not death or dying that frightened him, but the unexpected-
> ness of both. In sorting it all out, he hit on the notion that if
> one day a year were devoted to it, everybody could get it out
> of the way and the rest of the year would be safe and free. In
> this matter he instituted National Suicide Day.[21]

The first half of chapter two concerns eccentric Shadrack's precarious return to Medallion. Shadrack, as an eccentric character
who uses nonrational means, or any means, to protect his
human essentials, becomes a discursive fact that forms within *Sula*.

The second half of chapter two shows the neighborhood's response to Shadrack. Its first reaction to Shadrack and National

Suicide Day is one of fear—"At first the people in the town were frightened; they knew Shadrack was crazy but that did not mean that he didn't have any sense. . . ."[22] But a year later, its reaction changes from fear to "worrisome" and then to acceptance or tolerance: "Once the people understood the boundaries and nature of his madness, they could fit him, so to speak, into the scheme of things."[23]

The neighborhood's response to Shadrack reveals its flexibility in accepting and adapting to madness that is antithetical to the response that a rational, industrial society—a society whose social institutions have been permeated by technology and science and whose bodies of knowledge can only be explained rationally — would give. In rational, industrial societies where reason is hegemonic, madness is labeled a sickness, an aberration. Prior to the Age of Reason, Michel Foucault points out, madness was seen as "an undifferentiated experience, a not yet divided experience of division itself."[24]

In accepting Shadrack's madness as "an undifferentiated experience," *Sula* reproduces a "place" in time where the myraid human experiences—be they spiritual or mental—had not been divided completely: "As time went along, the people took less notice of these January thirds [National Suicide Days]. . . . In fact they had simply stopped remarking on the holiday because they had absorbed it into their thoughts, into their language, into their lives. . . . Easily, quietly, Suicide Day became a part of the fabric of life up in the Bottom of Medallion, Ohio."[25] Here we see how language incorporates and generalizes experiences as it produces a "reality" for the people of the Bottom. The neighborhood, as a vibrant and expansive place, becomes a second discursive fact that forms within the text.

Lévi-Strauss's *bricoleur* theory can assist in an explanation of *Sula's* infinite extension, its nonrational cosmology. In *The Savage Mind,* Lévi-Strauss compares the operation of the nonrational, nontechnical, nonliteral mind, whose thinking process he calls "mythical thought," to the *bricoleur* who "works with his hands and uses devious means compared to those of a craftsman."[26] The *bricoleur* uses the means at hand; that is, he uses instruments that are conceived for other purposes. He gives names and forms concepts for objects in their world solely in accordance with their needs:

> The characteristic feature of mythical thought is that it expresses itself by means of a heterogeneous repertoire. . . . It has to use this repertoire, however, whatever the task in hand because it has nothing at its disposal. Mythical thought is therefore a kind of intellectual 'bricolage'—which explains the relation which can be perceived between the two. . . . [It] builds up structured sets, not directly with other structured sets but by using the remains and debris of events. . . . Mythical thought for its part is imprisoned in the events and experiences which it never tires of ordering and re-ordering in its search to find them a meaning. But it also acts as a liberator by its protest against the idea that anything can be meaningless. . . .
>
> The mythical system and the modes of representations it employs serve to establish homologies between natural and social conditions or, more accurately, it makes it possible to equate significant contrasts found on different planes: the geographical, meterological, zoological, botanical, technical, economic, social, ritual, religious, and philosophical.[27]

Like the *bricoleur, Sula* allows the people of the Bottom to give names and form concepts for objects regardless of their plane. In other words, they use whatever is at hand to survive intellectually. This mode of survival is articulated in the Bottom's language as it defines reality.

As *Sula* progresses, the neighborhood, in its infinite extension, accepts and tolerates the middle-class and "proper" behavior of Helene Wright who seeks middle-class respectability to order her life and to protect her from her past, as well as from her own vulnerabilities: "Helene Wright was an impressive woman, at least in Medallion she was. Heavy hair in a bun, dark eyes arched in a perpetual query about other people's manners. A woman who won all social battles with presence and a conviction of the legitimacy of her authority."[28] As they do with Shadrack, the people of the Bottom accept and reinforce Helene's illusion of order and control. She becomes a reformulation of the discursive fact of the eccentric and extreme character who uses any means necessary to protect her own vulnerabilities and human essentials.

But in this reformulation of its two discursive categories, *Sula* establishes the conditions for their existence and their correlations with each other. The neighborhood is a resilient and flexible community whose social fabric allows its extreme and eccentric inhabitants to use nonrational means, or any means, to make sense out of their lives and the events that occur within their existence.

The fourth chapter—"1921"— introduces the Peace household, which gives further insight into the Bottom's cosmology and its inhabitants. Eva Peace, Sula's grandmother, "is arrogant, independent, decidedly a man lover who loves and hates intensely."[29] She is strong by virtue of her will, wit, and idiosyncrasies. That strength is nurtured and sustained by her hatred of BoyBoy, the unfaithful father of her three children. BoyBoy leaves Eva with "$1.65, five eggs, three beets and no idea of what or how to feel."[30] When he returns for a visit years later and never gets around to asking about their children, Eva knows that she "would hate him long." In hating BoyBoy, she knows that she could order her life, for her hatred of him would give her the "safety, the thrill, the consistency" she needs to define, strengthen, or protect her from "routine vulnerabilities."

Moreover the neighborhood's mythical system assists Eva in making sense out of her struggle for coherent meaning and survival. When she is hospitalized after trying to save her daughter Hannah from burning to death, Eva makes sense out of the fire that burned Hannah to death by remembering the "wedding dream" and recalling that "wedding always meant death." "The red gown," Eva thinks, "was the fire, as she should have known." Another instance of Eva's use of mythical thought is provided by the "plague of robins" that accompany Sula's return. When Sula enters Eva's house, Eva exclaims, "I might have knowed them birds meant something." Of course, Eva, in need of an explanation for Sula's return, associates this with the presence of the birds. Like other characters in *Sula* who need to make sense out of the events of their lives, Eva associates the human phenomenon of Sula's return with a natural symbol—the plague of robins. Eva is a repetition of the discursive fact of the extreme, uncommon, and eccentric character within the text.

The selection, arrangement, and reformulation of its discursive facts and categories permit *Sula* to make a particular statement, or produce a particular myth or representation, about the American and Afro-American historical past: after slavery and until the 1960s, black people, to survive their human conditions, produced a neighborhood that had an infinite extension. It was a neighborhood that came into existence as the result of a "nigger joke," that allowed its inhabitants—many of whom were eccentric and uncommon but not one-dimensional—to think their existence and explain the world satisfactorily by establishing homologies and analogies between the ordering of nature and that of society. It is a neighborhood that serves as a bulwark to protect its inhabitants' human essentials, their human vulnerabilities and frailties, against the dominant society's repression as well as against natural and human disasters. Within the neighborhood each member devises his own definition of existence without the pressure of conformity. Discussing elsewhere this Afro-American tolerance for differences, Morrison conjectures: "Black people have a way of allowing things to go on the way they're going. We're . . . not too terrified of being different, not too upset about divisions among things, people. Our interests have always been, it seems to me, on how un-alike things are rather than how alike things are. Black people always see differences before they see similarities."[31] This statement about the American and Afro-American violates dominant myths found in the works of Page, Twain, Faulkner, Richard Wright, and others. The Afro-American is not seen here as a docile, pathological victim who has deviated from dominant white norms. He or she is seen as different, as someone who belongs to a different cosmology, a different set of presuppositions. This statement also causes the reader to reformulate the text's essential question: why is the neighborhood that is expansive and flexible dissolving?

In succeeding chapters and years, *Sula* repeats and reformulates its discursive fact of the eccentric character in Tar Baby, Sula, and Hannah. In showing Tar Baby confronting death, the text repeats the discursive facts of the extreme, uncommon, and eccentric character and the flexible and expansive neighborhood. It also shows further correlations between these two discursive facts. Tar Baby is slowly drinking himself to death. Hannah shows an initial concern, but his death wish eventually becomes palpable to her, as well as to the other members of the Peace house and the community. They realize that Tar Baby "simply wanted a place to die privately but not quite alone." Also Tar Baby, like Eva and Shadrack, uses nonrational means to think his death wish coherently. He, along with the Deweys, is the first to join Shadrack on National Suicide Day. The neighborhood accepts and tolerates Tar Baby's differences.

But although Tar Baby's episode repeats the text's discursive facts, it also shows further correlations between them. The eccentric and uncommon character's action and behavior are not only tolerated and accepted by the neighborhood, they also lend credence, identity, and cohesion to the neighborhood. His actions provoke a response from the people. That provocation shows under what conditions these people make decisions about their lives, how they serve their intellectual needs, and how they make sense out of the human phenomena within their existence as they strive for equilibrium. The provocations show the people's response to certain human phenomena such as hate, death, evil, and fear.

Therefore, when the people up in the Bottom think that Tar Baby takes death too seriously, they do not interfere—as they do not interfere with Eva's hate or Helene's bourgeois manners. Instead they use his death wish as a way of reflecting upon and comprehending their own imminent death: "they just listened to him sing, wept and thought very graphically of their own imminent deaths. The people either accepted his own evaluation of his life, or were indifferent to it."[32] In taking death too seriously, Tar Baby, unlike the community, refuses to view death as a part of an "order from which nothing escapes." What is presupposed in the Bottom's cosmology is an unreserved acceptance of mortality. In their acceptance of death, some people of the Bottom accept life. This means that they are able to live every moment with the basic harmony or rationality of instinct in which life and death coexist. People like Sula and Ajax "make up themselves"; they are in constant touch with a fundamental reality of flux or pure becoming. The Bottom shows one of the ramifications of human mortality in a pre-Christian epoch. Defining the concept of death before the Age of Reason, Foucault writes: "where once man's madness had been not to see that death's term was approaching, so that it was necessary to recall him to wisdom with the spectacle of death, now [during the Age of Reason] wisdom consisted of denouncing madness everywhere, teaching men that they were no more than dead men already, and that if the end was near, it was to the degree that madness, become universal, would be one and the same with death itself."[33] For the Bottom, Tar Baby's death wish recalls them "to wisdom." It allows them to approach death's inevitability unscathed and orderly.

In continuing to generate its mythical thought representation of the American and Afro-American historical past and before it answers its question, *Sula* repeats its discursive facts in Hannah whose obsession with men and sex, but not "passion" and "commitment," functions to protect her from her own vulnerabilities and human frailties. It also demonstrates the community's response to sex. For Hannah sex is instinctual and natural; it is "pleasant and frequent, but otherwise unremarkable." It makes her "only happier."[34] Therefore, after her husband's death she has "a steady sequence of lovers, mostly the husbands of her friends and neighbors."[35] The people of the Bottom have varied responses to Hannah, but all responses are acceptable within the neighborhood's expansive cosmology. The women resent Hannah's sexual generosity, yet they accept her extremity and differences. Because Hannah is "unquestionably a kind and generous woman," the men defend and protect her.

Hannah also uses mythical thought to think coherently about events and phenomena in her life. For example, when Hannah has a dream of a "wedding in a red bridal gown," she searches for a natural or human phenomenon to explain the "red." Is it a sign of Sula's initiation into womanhood? Actually, the red bridal gown, along with the wind, presages Hannah's own death.

Finally, *Sula* repeats its discursive fact of the uncommon and extreme character in Sula. First, through commentary, the text defines evil in the Bottom's cosmology:

In spite of their fear, they reacted to an oppressive oddity,
or what they called evil days, with an acceptance that bor-
dered on welcome. Such evil must be avoided, they felt, and
precautions must naturally be taken to protect themselves
from it. But they let it run its course, fulfill itself, and never
invented ways either to alter it, to annihilate it or to prevent
its happening again. So also were they with people.

What was taken by outsiders to be slackness, slovenliness or
even generosity was in fact a full recognition of the legitimacy
of forces other than good ones. . . .

The purpose of evil was to survive it and they determined
. . . to survive floods, white people, tuberculosis, famine and
ignorance.[36]

The community's response to evil is similar to its previous responses to death, madness, and hate. It first expresses fear, then
absorbs, accepts, or tolerates. Second, it moves to make evil usa-
ble or functional in the way it thinks about its world.

Therefore, when Sula returns to Medallion after a ten-year absence, she comes to embody evil, for all of her actions are interpreted as sinister. The people of the Bottom call her a "roach"
when she puts Eva in Sunnydale, a home for the elderly, and respond nonrationally by laying "broomsticks across their doors at
night" and sprinkling "salt on porch steps." When the people
learn what Sula did to Nel's marriage—"she took Jude, then
ditched him for others"—they call her a "bitch." When the men
learn that Sula "slept with white men," they give her "the final
label." Other sinister deeds are attributed to Sula: she is accused
of pushing Teapot down the steps, causing Mr. Finley to choke
on a chicken bone and to die on the spot; coming to church supper "without underwear," and of not looking her age. Finally,
she is accused of getting Shadrack's attention.

Functionally, these nefarious deeds change the people of the
Bottom:

Their conviction of Sula's evil changed them in accountable
yet mysterious ways. Once the source of their personal misfortune was identified, they had leave to protect and love one an-

other. They began to cherish their husbands and wives, protect
their children, repair their homes and in general band together
against the devil in their midst. In their world, aberrations
were as much a part of nature as grace. It was not for them to
expel or annihilate it. They would no more run Sula out of
town than they would kill the robins that brought her back.[37]

Because "aberrations were a part" of their cosmology, they accept Sula's differences; they accept evil as one of the forces that
exist within the spectrum of human life. They use Sula to learn
who they are: she lends credence, identity, and cohesion to their
neighborhood.

But despite the fact that Shadrack, Eva, and others use the
Bottom to order and control their lives, to make sense out of the
events and human phenomena in their world, and to protect
their vulnerabilities and human frailties, ultimately they fail.
Their facades are jolted or proven inadequate, for the rigidity of
their facades is incongruent with the absurdity, possibility, prob-
ability, and ambiguity that characterize human life. Their facades do not allow for chance. For example, despite the fact that
Helene Wright marries an outsider, moves from New Orleans to
Medallion, Ohio, procures social respectability, and orders and
controls her own life to escape her mother's disputable life, she
fails to escape "all the old vulnerabilities, all the old fears."
When Helene boards the train to New Orleans for her grandmother's funeral, she, like her mother and grandmother, is
viewed as a sexual object. Despite her elegant wool dress and her
affected manners, she is viewed only as "custard." Seeing what
happens to her mother on the train, Nel begins to "make protective proscriptions of her own." But Nel's proscriptions, like her
mother's, ultimately fail her.

This illusion of protecting one's vulnerabilities and controlling
one's life against chance fails others in the community as well.
Even though Eva uses hate to order her life and to protect her
vulnerabilities, she cannot prevent Sula from putting her in a
home for the elderly. Jude, who is unable to acquire meaningful
employment, uses his marriage to Nel, which also fails, as a way
of being a man, of ordering his life. But he eventually leaves for

Detroit and an unstructured and precarious existence. Even
Shadrack, who wants to put a hand on death by instituting National Suicide Day, fails. The deaths of Plum, Chicken Little,
Hannah, and Sula do not happen on Shadrack's National Suicide
Day. In fact, the first time Shadrack begins "to suspect that all
those years . . . were never going to do any good," people of the
Bottom are killed in a tunnel on National Suicide Day. But despite the inadequacy of their facades, many of *Sula's* characters
survive. Helene Wright lives to marry off her daughter and to
become an old woman. Although she is placed in a nursing
home, Eva lives into her nineties. At the close of the text in
1965, Nel, Ajax, and Shadrack are still alive.

At the end of *Sula* when the "unfinished tunnel" collapses, the
Bottom is no longer the same kind of neighborhood that it was
in 1919, with an infinite extension to accept and to make sense
out of the diverse human characters and situations that span the
spectrum of human existence. Events occur between 1941 and
1965 that cause a transformation and the inevitable collapse of
"that place." In 1941 Sula was the last force to give the members
of the neighborhood something to "rub up against" as they
sought identity, credence, and cohesion. After Sula's death Medallion turns "silver" and the people display their "personal mis-
fortunes," for "without her mockery, affection for others sank
into flaccid disrepair." But the disintegration of this community
began much earlier: "As soon as the silvering began, long before
the cider cracked the jugs, there was something wrong. A falling
away, a dislocation was taking place."[38] Daughters put their
mothers in homes for the elderly; mothers no longer defend or
care for their children; and "wives uncoddled their husbands."
Also, blacks begin teaching in the schools of Medallion and
"working in the dime store." Middle-class blacks emerged as a
distinct group. Members of this once communal neighborhood
begin to live in "separate houses with separate televisions and
separate telephones and less and less dropping by."[39] This once
culturally self-sufficient neighborhood becomes dependent upon
organized, industrial society for life sustenance and food. When
Teapot asks his mother for "sugar-butter-bread," she gives him
"olemargarin" and "saffron-colored powder."

These textual events signify an extraliteralary transformation that was occurring in the dominant society and that would contribute to the eventual collapse of the Bottom. Between 1941 and 1965 the United States became one of the most economically prosperous countries in the world. Much of this prosperity was due to advances in science and technology that after 1945 permeated and organized successfully the entire American society, including those nonrational, nonliteral, and nontechnical segregated pockets of Afro-American neighborhoods. This period also witnessed the emergence of the civil rights movement, which fought—successfully in the courts—segregated laws that had barred blacks from participating in the social and economic arenas of the country.

This transformation affected the Bottom community where its middle-class blacks "who had made money during the war moved as close as they could to the valley." These middle-class blacks, in aspiring for the same individualistic goals and ambitions as the members of the dominant American society, initiated the transition of the Bottom from a nonliteral, nontechnical, and mythical society to an industrial, rational, and individualistic society. In an interview with Ntozake Shange in the *American Rag,* Morrison discusses the disappearance of the black neighborhood: "It's our fault—it might be industrialization—but my generation didn't tell somebody something. We had a long period of aspiration to the middle class in which the important thing was not to remember the sharecropper grandfather, to blot that out because that was sullying in the press towards respectability, money and so on."[40] With greater economic and political opportunities, these middle-class blacks begin not only to move into the industrial society but also to adopt and practice the values, definitions, and life styles of the dominant culture.

In this social and economic transformation, the people's traditional "intelligence," their "resilience," their "wide-spirited celebrations of life," their care for the welfare of others, and their "infinite tolerance for differences" are lost. Even the "modern-day whores" who are "clothes crazy" adopt the soft values of the dominant bourgeois society. They do not possess the stamina and fortitude of those "silvery widows in the woods who would

get up from the dinner table and walk into the trees with a cus-
tomer with as much embarrassment as a calving mare."[41]

Last, and perhaps most important, in a more general way the
Bottom is transformed because it is "imprisoned in the events
and experiences which it tires of ordering and re-ordering in its
search to find" meaning. Although the Bottom's cosmology "acts
as a liberator by its protest against the idea that anything can be
meaningless," it does not provide the neighborhood with the intellectual rigor to discriminate, to assess critically its internal
"events," "experiences," and the external rational forces that act
upon it. Its lack of grasping rationality causes the Bottom to dis-
solve. Unable to withstand the rigor of the dominant society, the
community portrayed in *Sula* comes full circle since its collapse
or devastation at the end is actually its beginning.

But exactly what about this produced American and Afro-
American historical past did *Sula* want to show us? What does it
show us about the historical past that other representations do
not? First, it shows the tremendous price its inhabitants must
pay to survive. Because they are preoccupied with protecting
their vulnerabilities, the characters become egocentric. They
never have the opportunities to assert their individualities, to
tap their human potentials and possibilities, and to explore the
borders of their lives. To keep his life focused and ordered,
Shadrack devotes all of his energies to fishing, drinking, cleaning
house, and presiding over National Suicide Day. He has no time
or inclination to explore other interests or himself, to seek com-
panionship, or to think of wanting children. Because their lives
are preoccupied with attaining social respectability, neither
Helene nor Nel gets around to exploring other dimensions of
their lives. (Nel however does begin to raise certain questions
near the end of the text.)

Even those characters who leave Medallion in search of hope,
a better life, and personal fulfillment are left unfulfilled. After
BoyBoy leaves her destitute with three children, Eva leaves Medallion for eighteen months and returns sagacious and haughty.
When her house is complete, she moves in and rules it like a
god. She sits "in a wagon on the third floor directing the lives of
her children, friends, strays, and a constant stream of board-

ers."[42] But although she is "sovereign" and "creator" of this "enormous house," Eva is never able to express love to her children in a way that they can understand it. When Hannah asks Eva if she loves them, Eva replies, "You settin' here with your healthy-ass self and ax me did I love you? Them big old eyes in your head would a been two holes full of maggots if I hadn't. . . . Play? Wasn't nobody playin' in 1895. Just 'cause you got it good now you think it was always this good? 1895 was a killer, girl. Things was bad. . . . What would I look like leapin' 'round that little old room playin' with youngins with three beets to my name."[43] Because Eva is preoccupied with daily survival, she has had no time to "play" and cuddle her children.

Neither BoyBoy nor Plum is able to live a full life. After five years of "a sad and disgruntled marriage," BoyBoy leaves Medallion. But a brief visit shows that his travels have not brought him happiness and fulfillment: "Underneath all of that shine she [Eva] saw defeat in the stalk of his neck and the curious tight way he held his shoulders."[44] Plum finds himself in a similar predicament. After getting out of the army in 1919, he wanders from New York to Washington to Chicago "full of promises of homecomings, but there was obviously something wrong."

Sula likewise leaves Medallion and returns ten years later unfulfilled, independent, evil, and still unconventional. She wanders from Nashville to Detroit to New Orleans to New York to Philadelphia to Macon to San Diego in search of fulfillment, in search of that part of her that would give her substance, understanding, excitement, and wholeness. All she finds is "boredom."

All those cities held the same people, working the same mouths, sweating the same sweat. The men who took her to one or another of those places had merged into one large personality: the same language of love, the same entertainments of love, the same cooling of love. . . .

In a way, her strangeness, her naiveté, her craving for the other half of her equation was the consequence of an idle imagination. Had she paints, or clay, or knew the discipline of the dance, or strings; had she anything to engage her tremendous curiosity and her gift for a metaphor, she might have ex-

changed the restlessness and preoccupation with whim for an
activity that provided her with all she yearned for. And like
any artist with no art form, she became dangerous.[45]

Therefore she returns to Medallion, hoping to find "the other
half of her equation" in Nel.

These complex characters such as Sula, Eva, Plum, and BoyBoy
are alienated, alone, and unfulfilled; they are, to use Morrison's
term, "outdoors"—"Outdoors, we knew, was the real terror of
life. . . . If you are put out, you go somewhere else; if you are outdoors, there is no place to go."[46] The image of such characters in
the Afro-American historical past is excluded in most dominant
American and Afro-American myths about that past.

Sula's representation of the American and Afro-American historical past shows black men as victims of oppression. Unable to
find employment and his niche in society, BoyBoy preoccupies
himself "with other women. . . . He did whatever he could that
he liked, and he liked womanizing best, drinking second, and
abusing Eva third."[47] Also displaced and abandoned by the society are the "old men and young ones" who "draped themselves
in front of the Elmira Theater, Irene's Palace of Cosmetology,
the pool hall, the grill and the other sagging business enterprises
that lined the street. On sills, on stoops, on crates and broken
chairs they sat tasting their teeth and waiting for something to
distract them."[48]

Even Ajax, a free spirit, is limited by oppression. Unable to
pursue his second love, airplanes, Ajax takes "long trips" to
"large cities" and leans against the barbed wire of airports "to
hear the talk of the men who were fortunate enough to be in the
trade." Other times he watches his mother's magic or he spends
his time "in the idle pursuits of bachelors without work in small
towns." With Ajax, as with Sula, Morrison shows us how oppression and limitations stifle growth, abort potentials, and cause the
individual to live an idle life.

Sula shows other ways the Afro-American in the historical
past made sense out of his existence—ways that are excluded
from other dominant American representations. Morrison uses
dreams, myths, and superstitions as accepted verities, as estab-

lished cultural forms, as knowing references. Weddings and dreams that presage death and foretell the future, weather that symbolizes human phenomena, and human events and phenomena that are explained by natural phenomena are accepted as part of the Bottom's cosmology, as part of the neighborhood's stock knowledge.

Finally, this produced American and Afro-American historical past in *Sula* makes it possible for the text to show how black women reinvent themselves and provide a support system for each other. Since both Sula and Nel have had similar experiences of being black, female, lonely, and the only children in the family, they understand each other immediately:

> So when they met . . . they felt the ease and comfort of old friends. Because each had discovered years before that they were neither white nor male, and that all freedom and triumph was forbidden to them, they had set about creating something else to be. Their meeting was fortunate, for it let them use each other to grow on. Daughters of distant mothers and incomprehensible fathers . . . they found in each other's eyes the intimacy they were looking for.[49]

As friends, Sula and Nel are able to complement each other. While they are young—before Nel gets married and Sula leaves town—the two provide the sustenance and the "other half" for each other. Sula helps Nel define herself. When they are older, they still need each other. When Nel comes to grips with Jude's infidelity, she wants to talk to Sula, but Sula is the culprit. When Sula is dying and finds it does not hurt, she thinks to tell Nel. Although sexual betrayal breaks up this friendship, years later Nel realizes that her loneliness was not due to Jude's absence, but to Sula's:

> "Sula?" she whispered, gazing at the tops of trees.
> "Sula?". . . .
> "All that time, all that time, I thought I was missing Jude." And the loss pressed down on her chest and came up into her throat. "We was girls together," she said as though explaining something. "O Lord, Sula," she cried, "girl, girl, girlgirlgirl."[50]

This friendship between Nel and Sula reproduces in the Afro-American historical past a phenomenon—the image of black women as complex human beings who are capable of the kind of bond traditionally associated with men—that is excluded from all pre-sixties representations of the Afro-American historical past. Here we see how Morrison's feminist concern about the historical representation of black women informs the production of *Sula.*

But to show this representation of the American and Afro-American historical past, *Sula* has to be silent on other representations of that historical past. It is silent on other ways the Afro-American in the historical past responded to racial oppression. Unlike Sula, Jude, and Ajax, some Afro-Americans from the historical past were able to channel their creative talents and energies into various artistic endeavors—such as writing, singing, gardening, quilting, and preaching. Stagolee Dupas in Murray's *Train Whistle Guitar* channels his frustrations into music. Other Afro-Americans were able to forge their creative talents and intellectual acumen into various political activities—such as organizing the community, or sabotaging or interrupting society's "natural" process. Ned Douglass and Jimmy Aaron in Gaines's *The Autobiography of Miss Jane Pittman* defy the status quo because they find it dehumanizing. Rather than be content with surviving and protecting their vulnerabilities and human frailties, they organize politically. Still other Afro-Americans in the historical past were able to channel their frustrations and aggressions into educational endeavors—building schools or getting an education.

To show these options, *Sula* would counter its intention of showing those Afro-Americans who, because they did not have sufficient outlets, became uncommon, egocentric, and extreme in their behaviors, actions, and obsessions. These options are statements that *Sula's* discursive formation denies.

Thus, in describing *Sula's* corpus of discursive facts, in making salient its gaps and silences, we can discern how it—like Gaines's *The Autobiography of Miss Jane Pittman,* Walker's *The Third Life of Grange Copeland,* and Murray's *Train Whistle Guitar*—is a discourse informed by larger philosophical and ideological constraints, such as magic or the surreal, feminism, an Afro-American mythical (folk) thought system, or a particular audience. We see how *Sula* functions as a cultural object—creating a myth about the American and Afro-American histori-cal past for a particular audience by incorporating certain cate-gories and systems of concepts that inform the reader's expectations. How *Sula* is received, which is discussed in the final chapter, is contingent on how many of these categories and systems of concepts—and the lived experience they produce—can be appropriated by mainstream critics, reviewers, and the like.

As a discourse, *Sula* has its own strategies, along with its gaps and silences, to make speak its enunciation. These strategies, gaps, and silences are evident when we examine how Sula, along with the other three texts discussed, defines and interprets phe-nomena from the American and Afro-American historical past. For example, *The Third Life* interprets the black male as being passive, brutal, emotionless, and violent. *Miss Jane Pittman* and *Train Whistle Guitar* interpret him as heroic, legendary, and very affirmative. *Train Whistle Guitar* interprets black life and culture as a blues life where individuals confront, acknowledge, and proceed with life in spite of the "ugliness and meanness in-herent in the human condition." *The Third Life* interprets that same black life and culture as being pathological. It presents black life and culture as victimized by the oppressive dominant system, as having no will beyond what is permitted by the system.

Both *Sula* and *The Autobiography of Miss Jane Pittman* have different interpretations of the sixties' movement. In *Miss Jane Pittman,* as in *The Third Life,* the sixties are interpreted as the release of new energies, as the psychological and physical libera-tion from a constricting social system. But *Sula* shows the sixties as a loss—a time when blacks are "distracted from what is wor-thy" about them, when they lose the sustenance that had allowed them to survive the hardships of America.

In delineating how the various Afro-American texts of the 1960s and 1970s reproduce different representations of the American and Afro-American historical past, we see how that historical past is not one continuous development centered around one object. We see how the American and Afro-

American historical past is not one truth, but many; not one real experience, but many realities; not one history, but many different and valid ways of looking at and interpreting events. The American and Afro-American historical past is a series of discursive formations that are not necessarily linked, but that give different interpretations of categories and facts.

The crucial question is: if there is an established American and Afro-American historical past that is the product of one continuous development, why do *Sula, Miss Jane Pittman, The Third Life of Grange Copeland,* and *Train Whistle Guitar* interpret the sixties, black culture, black manhood differently? Is there a greater, a universal, model to measure these representations of the American and Afro-American historical past? What we can deduce is that representations of the American and Afro-American historical past have more to do with discursive formations, with individuals' and groups' subjective conditions and their needs to define the historical past to validate and make coherent those conditions, to ratify the present and to indicate directions for the future, than they have to do with a "real" American and Afro-American historical past. In short, our readings and interpretations of the historical past are vitally dependent on our experience of the present.

Thus, the American social movement of the 1960s produced the option for the Afro-American to move to the exteriority of the dominant ideological apparatus and for the reemergence of excluded American and Afro-American discursive formations such as cultural nationalism, feminism, omni-Americanism. With this option, Afro-American writers such as Alice Walker, Ernest J. Gaines, Albert Murray, Toni Morrison, and others produced new kinds of Afro-American texts that violated the safe, passive literary image of the Afro-American. They produced texts that strained the ability of dominant generic techniques to effect a closure within their discursive formations.

The crucial question now is how are these Afro-American texts of the 1960s and 1970s that produced Other, different representations of the American and Afro-American historical past defined and interpreted by the dominant society's literary establishment? by Afro-American cultural, nationalist, and feminist critics? What happened to the image of the Afro-American and the Afro-American text in post-sixties America? Are new strategies being devised by the dominant American ideological apparatus to appropriate these sixties and seventies texts, to regain control of the image of the Afro-American? The next chapter will attempt to answer these questions.

Chapter 8. The Post-Sixties, the Ideological Apparatus, and the Afro-American Text

In their challenge to the dominant American ideological apparatus, the American social movements of the 1960s forced the political, social, educational, and cultural institutions and practices within the ideological apparatus to become more flexible and expansive. These institutions had to accommodate the Other. The political arena opened to include more black elected officials. Predominantly white American colleges and universities enrolled larger numbers of black students. The corporate and business world, along with the media institutions, became more sensitive to the historical exclusion of blacks and other minorities. Within the cultural apparatus, the literary institutions—publishing houses, editors, review journals and magazines, granting and awarding agencies, and English departments—became more aware of the exclusion of Afro-American literature.

This expansion of literary institutions caused a change in the literary and ideological forces that produce Afro-American texts. It gave Afro-American writers the option to write new kinds of Afro-American texts, to produce *different* Afro-American images that burst asunder the prevailing images of the Afro-American. But an examination of dominant American literary institutions' response to these new Afro-American texts and images informs us that the cultural apparatus expanded as a result of the sixties' movements, but it did not change its goals, values, assumptions, and basic suppositions.

To regain control over these sixties rebellious elements that
challenged its hegemony, the ideological apparatus altered system elements and produced some marginal options, thereby producing space for a *token* inclusion of the Afro-American within
its discursive formation, its ideological apparatus. But this inclusion did not mean that a transformation had taken place in the
discursive formation of the dominant ideological apparatus to
allow for the incorporation or acceptance of the Other on its
own terms. Rather, the incorporation of the Afro-American as
the Other meant a redefinition or appropriation of the Afro-
American to make him or her appear safe and "natural." What
other strategies were used to regain control over the sixties rebellious elements?

In *The End of Prosperity,* Harry Magdoff and Paul Sweezy
argue that as the United States approached the 1970s, it was
coming to the end of a long period of economic prosperity—the
decades between the 1940s and the early 1970s during which
capital accumulation on a global scale proceeded with unprece-
dented vigor. The period was characterized by relatively long cy-
clical upswings and mild recessions.[1] Magdoff and Sweezy contend further that the continuing post-World War II war deficit
was caused by the huge foreign exchange cost of controlling a
world: that is, putting war-torn capitalist countries on their feet,
and maintaining military bases around the world. The costs of
running an international empire were sharply inflated by the ex-
pensive Vietnam War. Also, the United States trade surplus
began to dwindle under the impact of domestic inflation and
tougher European and Japanese competition for export markets.[2]

As a result of these rather costly adventures, the United States
economy was plagued with inflation and the middle class in
America found itself in an economic crisis. Because of inflation,
this middle class's standard of living declined. The economic crisis produced a crisis in the American sociocultural system. One
consequence was that the American middle class was not as generous in the late seventies and early eighties as it was in the late
sixties and early seventies in supporting Afro-American, women's,
and minority "gains." Instead, it led the revolt to revoke many
of those concessions that had been made by the dominant Amer-

ican society in the late sixties and early seventies. Many middle-class Americans, believed, for example, that blacks had achieved an equality with their white counterparts. The effects of this economic and sociocultural crisis were the erosion of the relative tolerance, diversity, pluralism, and freedom that had permitted the development of alternative programs not only for blacks and other minorities but also for the dominant American society.

In adjusting to this economic crisis and in bringing these subversive sixties elements back into its fold, the dominant ideological apparatus began to absorb, transform, and incorporate these elements. As Afro-Americans of the sixties began to strike their eminently marketable poses, as their vocabulary, speech, gestures, ideas, and values became more familiar, the context to which they could be most conveniently assigned was made increasingly apparent. The media not only recorded Afro-Americans' resistance to normative conventions and values but situated their resistance within the dominant society's framework. Afro-Americans' goals and intentions—as well as their lethal attacks on the dominant society's oppression, contradictions, and injustice—were placed where common sense, as defined by the dominant society, would have them fit. In short, many of Afro-American goals and intentions—especially those that threatened the hegemony of the dominant society—were sabotaged and appropriated.

The appropriation or redefinition of the Afro-American's resistance took many forms. The media projected sixties black militants as being angry, violent, haters of whites, and incorrect ideologically. The motivation for the militant rhetoric and behavior was excluded. The image of black militants was drained of their genuine struggle against racial oppression, their challenge to the dominant American society, and was filled with or transformed into an irrational entity or image where they were made to look extreme and preposterous. Episode after episode of television programs such as "Starsky and Hutch," "Police Woman," "Baretta," and other police programs that abounded in the seventies discredited the genuine plight of angry, militant Afro-Americans.

Many of the sixties Afro-American styles, which showed the

Afro-American's values or ideological differences from the dominant society, were incorporated and naturalized. The buba-
wearing, hip-talking, Afro-wearing militant was dressing one
value system but was talking another: going to Harvard Business
School, talking about "black capitalism," and getting his piece of
the American pie. The "natural" hair style lost its signal of rejection of the normative and became just another American fad.
American presidents and politicians began to talk "hip" and to
give the "soul" handshake. What started out as ways to
delegitimate the ruling social order were absorbed and incorporated by that system.

Within the literary establishment, institutions began to reassert
their practices of appropriating Afro-American texts and of assessing and defining Afro-American texts according to how closely they reproduce normative literary values, subjects, themes,
and perspectives. First, the National Endowment for the Humanities, with conservative director William Bennett and a re-
duced budget, retreated from supporting innovative research
projects, including ethnic and feminist studies. Conservative
scholars riding the Reagan election to power were insisting on a
"pure" approach to the humanities, an approach "unsullied by
the multiracial, multisexual perspectives of contemporary . . .
life."[3] In short, Bennett returned an Anglo-American (male) conception of culture to center stage in American research. The
move by the National Endowment for the Humanities began af-
fecting universities and the kinds of research that were being
funded.[4] This return to an Anglo-American (male) conception of
culture does not mean that no Afro-American scholars were
funded by the National Endowment for the Humanities. Rather,
it means that to be funded their proposals had to reflect this
"pure" approach to the humanities. They had to research those
subjects deemed worthy by these newly reemergent conservative
scholars. Their proposals had to be overwhelmingly positivistic,
empirical, and nationalistic (American), for the Endowment was
excluding systematically nonempirical and nonpositivistic
proposals (such as semiotics, contemporary Marxism, and
hermeneutics).

Also, by the late 1970s, American universities, with Harvard at the forefront, saw the need for a more rigorous and structured humanities curriculum. They began reestablishing humanities core and Western civilization courses and making them breadth requirements. But in examining these core courses, we find that they resemble in content the old requirements. We find traditional canonical white male "classics" or "great books" regaining hegemony, with a token female, minority, or Marxist text included. The sixties elective system, which had brought a pluralism to the humanities, was forced to the margins.[5] In short, humanities core courses and Western civilization courses became counter-revolution against the elective system of which black studies, ethnic studies, and women studies were a part.

In their expansion during the sixties English departments included courses in "black literature," "Asian literature," "Native American literature," and "Chicano literature." But they rarely questioned or altered the discursive formation or the ideological base that produced the traditional American canon. English departments rarely questioned or altered their existing "traditional" courses. The aesthetic assumptions about what constitutes "great" literature remains white, male, and upper-middle-class with token gestures to those Other American texts that reproduced many of the established literary conventions, as well as the predominant defined literary experience. As David Bradley so eloquently points out in "Black and American, 1982," English departments continue to advertise a course in "American" fiction that explicitly includes "Hawthorne, Clemens, James, Wharton, Hemingway, Fitzgerald, and Faulkner" and implicitly excludes Chesnutt, Hurston, Wright, Himes, Ellison, Okada, Momaday, and Kingston.[6] They continue to advertise a course in "American" poetry that includes Whitman, Dickinson, Frost, Pound, Eliot, Stevens, Williams, Moore, Lowell, and Plath and excludes Dunbar, Hughes, Brooks, Hayden, Baraka, Margaret Walker, and Sterling Brown. The point is not that English departments should not offer a fiction course that includes Hawthorne, Clemens, and James, but that it should call the course what it is—a course in white American male writers.

As for the dominant literary institutions' response to Afro-American texts of the sixties and seventies, they reasserted their

censorship and exclusion. By the late seventies many major publishing houses were back to publishing only two black books a
year, if that many. Commenting on this return to normalcy,
June Jordan writes: "At the end of the 1960s, American mass
media rolled the cameras away from Black life and the quantity
of print on the subject became too small to read. As a result, the
number of books published by and about Black people has been
neglible since the beginning of this decade."[7] During the seventies review journals and magazines slowly reemerged to define
what constitutes "good" literature. Normative criticism returned
to determine the worth of Afro-American texts in accordance to
their contribution to a defined body of "knowledge." It certified
those Afro-American texts judged to speak the discourse better;
and, as is the nature of discourse, it excludes those texts, subjects, and perspectives that do not conform—thereby effecting
silences, again, in American literature.

But in the late sixties and early seventies, many Afro-
American and feminist critics no longer accepted normative criticism as "natural." They established their own aesthetic standards and criteria, different from those of the dominant
American literary practices, for judging and assessing the worth
and value of Afro-American and feminist texts. On a limited
scale, they established their own apparatuses—journals and magazines, university course offerings, conferences, departments,
programs, and research centers, etc.—to counter the co-optation
and appropriation of Afro-American and feminist texts. But exactly how did mainstream reviewers and critics appropriate sixties and seventies Afro-American texts? How did Afro-American
and feminist critical practices counter this appropriation—this
forcing of feminist and Afro-American texts to speak the single
literary voice of established American literature?

In their discussions of Gaines's *The Autobiography of Miss
Jane Pittman,* mainstream reviewers write of *Miss Jane
Pittman's* similarities to other "great" texts within the dominant
literary establishment, its "aesthetic distance that characterizes
the classic American writer," or they emphasize Miss Jane as a
"legendary figure" and place her within the tradition of other
"great works." But these critics and reviewers exclude any dis-

cussion of *Miss Jane Pittman's* Other representation of the American and Afro-American historical past. They exclude any examination of those *different,* nonconformist subjects and perspectives—such as Ned Douglass and Jimmy Aaron—that exist outside dominant literary myths and conventions. But, as I discussed in the chapter on Gaines, several Afro-American nationalist critics focus on *Miss Jane Pittman's* Other qualities that challenge and violate the standard myth about the Afro-American—thereby exposing what Guy Debord calls the "spectacle" that had come to represent the Other, the directly lived Afro-American experience.[8]

Alice Walker's *The Third Life of Grange Copeland* receives not appropriation but exclusion. It fails to reproduce sufficient literary conventions. Conventional reviewers and critics interpret *The Third Life* not as an "artistic creation" but as a sociological document. In his review in *Freedomways,* Loyle Hairston, echoing the reflectionist literary convention, writes: "*The Third Life* is a novel about how a degrading social existence imposed by the racist American plantation system often succeeded in debasing the lives of its victims and destroying their humanity."[9] In the *New Yorker,* Robert Coles, who later argues that Walker turns "dry sociological facts into a whole and alive particular person rather than a bundle of problems and attitudes," comments: "We all know that America's cities are in trouble, especially because blacks have fled to them in mixed hope and fear. . . . But almost no one has tried to tell us about the early lives, the *inner* early lives, of black people, the particular ways that black children in a rural setting grow, only to leave and become the urban poor. . . . The tragedy had to be documented."[10]

When interpreted as sociological documentation, *The Third Life* loses all those artistic qualities—style, "universality," textual strategies, literary modes—that the institutions within the dominant literary establishment deem necessary for greatness and endurance. These absent virtues are echoed in Mark Schorer's rather favorable review:

> She [Walker] is not a finished novelist. She has much to learn. Fortunately, what she has to learn are the unimportant les-

sons, that is, those that *can* be learned: some economy, formal shaping, stylistic tightening, deletion of points too repetitiously insisted upon, the handling of time, above all development rather than mere reversal of character. The important fictional qualities that she commands, those that she was born with, she has supremely. . . . *The Third Life of Grange Copeland* has a certain temporal progress . . . no developing struggle, only fits and starts.[11]

Schorer's comments imply certain underlying ideological assumptions about literature and aesthetic beauty. To be a "finished novelist" requires certain skills in craft that are tied to a certain definition of aesthetic beauty. But what Schorer calls the "unimportant lessons" that can be learned are really the standards and criteria used to judge whether or not a text is "good" literature. What is most critical about these critics' responses to *The Third Life* is that none of them sees the need to place it within the context or the tradition of American literature, thereby sending signals to English departments, granting agencies, and awarding agencies about its worth and value. These critics' and reviewers' interpretation of the text means that it is not their kind of literature.

As is the case of Gaines's *The Autobiography of Miss Jane Pittman, The Third Life* reaches into the nineteenth century for its literary genre—which has its own physiognomy, its own built-in themes, problems, and resolutions that do not explain adequately certain contemporary lived experiences encountered by contemporary readers and reviewers. Although these mostly white critics can sympathize with Grange's struggle for integrity and freedom and the women's suffering, these problems and issues have no immediacy in terms of their own lives. Because *The Third Life* uses a nineteenth-century genre to articulate a twentieth century problem, it might be deemed "immature" by certain critics and reviewers who would argue that the reality, problems, and resolutions *The Third Life* offers do not encompass and approximate the complexity of the twentieth-century historical condition. Therefore, these normative critics and reviewers interpret *The Third Life* distantly. They see Walker doing something with "dry sociological facts"; they interpret the text as being not about them, but "about the early lives, the *inner* early lives of black people."

Also, these normative reviewers ignore *The Third Life's* Other qualities; they exclude a discussion of Grange's education and transformation that allow him to transcend and *critique* the definitions, conventions, and images of the ruling social order and to talk of a new social order where he and Ruth are normative.

When *The Third Life* is interpreted in the feminist and Afro-American constellations where a different kind of literature exists, its value and worth are enhanced. Several Afro-American and feminist writers and critics, along with mainstream white male critics and reviewers who accept and embrace feminism because it explains certain valid contemporary lived experiences, write of Grange's Otherness, his education and transformation and vision. Trudier Harris writes of the profound Afro-American vision Walker brings to *The Third Life.*[12] Speaking about *The Third Life's* greatness, Nikki Giovanni comments that "that book comes down to Grange, the father, who has to decide that Brownfield is not worth living. Before he will let Brownfield destroy the future, he will kill him.... Now that was a hell of a statement Alice made."[13] David Bradley, in acknowledging and giving validity to the traditional and mainstream reviews of *The Third Life,* sees a greatness in the text. He writes: "Unlike a number of reviewers, I was even more taken with Alice Walker's first novel.... there is much to admire, especially in the 'third life,' in which Grange Copeland emerges as one of the richest, wisest and most moving old men in fiction."[14]

The Third Life will endure and have social and cultural value as long as there are feminist and Afro-American sociocultural contexts that have the powers to maintain it. Its wide acclaim can be attributed to these two sociocultural contexts. Otherwise, because it lacks certain themes and concerns that most mainstream critics deem important to merit literary recognition and that would allow them to situate the text within their own contemporary and traditional constellations, *The Third Life* will not find a place in the dominant American literary establishment as it is currently constituted.

Albert Murray's *Train Whistle Guitar* receives approbation similar to that given to *Miss Jane Pittman.* It, like *Miss Jane Pittman,* reproduces many of the literary conventions—the existential search, stream-of-consciousness technique, local color, etc.—of Faulkner, Mann, and Joyce. First, traditional critics and reviewers accent the text's similarity to other texts they have deemed "great." They praise *Train Whistle Guitar* for producing a literary experience that is in the tradition of Faulkner, Twain, and Sherwood Anderson. Thomas P. Edwards, of the *New York Review of Books,* places *Train Whistle Guitar* within the tradition of American fiction: "Murray's episodic fictional memoir of a black childhood and youth in Gasoline Point, Alabama in the 1920s doesn't wholly resist the temptation to settle for local color, the nostalgia for the pleasures of childhood in a protective rural setting that American fiction, good and bad, has always been ready to celebrate."[15] Within the American tradition, the text echoes the "local color" of Twain's *Huckleberry Finn* and the works of William Faulkner. It also echoes the works of Sherwood Anderson, Willa Cather, and Mark Twain in its "nostalgia for the pleasures of childhood in a protective rural setting." The reviewer for the *New Yorker* writes: "Mr. Murray (or Scooter) speaks a highly mannered tongue—a hybrid of Joyce, Faulkner, and Negro hyperbole."[16] *Book World*'s reviewer comments: "Murray's small town South is as perfectly and as personally captured as the larger worlds of Joyce, Faulkner, or Proust."[17] Because these reviewers and critics emphasize how *Train Whistle Guitar* reproduces certain established literary themes, stereotypes, and conventions and is, therefore, in the same tradition as Joyce, Faulkner, and Anderson, it becomes quite visible. It was sold into paperback and was distributed widely. It won the Lillian Smith Award for Southern fiction in 1974.

But, except for James Alan McPherson, mainstream critics and reviewers do not discuss *Train Whistle Guitar's* Otherness, its people and community who have the intellectual acumen to outmaneuver the whites in determining which images of the Afro-American will appear. These traditional critics do not discuss the text's alternative, blues style definition of existence that is as complex and sophisticated as, and certainly less stifling than, the dominant society's definition of existence. To discuss this Other in *Train Whistle Guitar* would force these mainstream critics to engage the limitations and constraints of the dominant society. Therefore, they exclude or ignore this Other.

Finally, Toni Morrison's *Sula* is also appropriated and seen as reproducing certain dominant literary myths. Reviewers like Colette Dowling and Diane Johnson seized immediately the opportunity to discuss *Sula*'s "primitivism," its violence, and its nonrational way of defining and thinking existence. They discuss *Sula* in terms of its differences. Emphasizing differences in a literary discourse that demands a single voice is, perhaps, the best way to contribute to a text's short life. The critics and reviewers never place *Sula* within the tradition of American literature. They never discuss *Sula's* Otherness, its articulation of another definition of existence in the Afro-American historical past, outside those definitions of the dominant society, where people have the freedom to live multifaceted lives. Instead, they interpret it in the same way that they interpret Hurston's *Their Eyes Were Watching God*—as the primitive, as exotica.

But *Sula* endures because it has entered the feminist and Afro-American discursive formations whose literary theories presuppose different uses of the text. They appropriate the text to reproduce their own discourses, their own ideological concerns and interests. For example, in *Black Women Novelists* Christian appropriates *Sula* into a feminist constellation by emphasizing one of its feminist categories: "In *Sula* . . . Morrison again takes on an apparently simple theme, the friendship of two black girls. One, Nel Wright, follows the pattern of life society has laid out for her, and the other, Sula Peace, tries to create her pattern, to achieve her own self."[18] As long as these discourses have the power to produce a reading audience, *Sula* will endure. Otherwise, the dominant American critical institutions have failed to impute to it any literary qualities.

Just as normative criticism moved to reestablish its hegemony over Afro-American texts, awarding agencies returned to placing accolades on particular kinds of Afro-American texts. In 1978, James Alan McPherson's *Elbow Room* received the Pulitzer Prize for fiction. In examining its reviews and its paucity of criticism, we can only discern that the book received the prize because it, either consciously or unconsciously, reproduced standard and expected literary themes and perspectives. The *Antioch Review* sees McPherson as a "writer who cannot be faulted with the form. It is incidental that the stories are about blacks."[19] In its review of *Elbow Room,* the *New York Times Book Review* describes it as a "dozen short stories by a highly gifted writer. They concern a diverse group of contemporary Americans who are determined to protect their individuality against the pressure of others."[20] In the *New York Review of Books,* Diane Johnson says that "in the stories of James Alan McPherson the ordinary white reader will at first feel at home. There are some men's magazine tall tales about romantic barroom types . . . which could have been written by any American with an ear for dialect and a satirical gift."[21] All these reviewers are preoccupied with stressing *Elbow Room*'s similarities to other established and legitimate literary themes and perspectives. Anything racial or different about McPherson's stories is played down.

In reviewing Toni Morrison's *Song of Solomon* (1977) which won the National Book Critics Circle Award, because the text reproduces many of the established literary themes and perspectives—such as the marginal youth looking for a home—the *New York Times* (daily) places the novel in the same category with Nabokov's *Lolita,* Heller's *Catch 22,* Lessing's *The Golden Notebook,* and Marquez's *One Hundred Years of Solitude.*[22]

In both of the above instances, the meaning and interpretation of *Elbow Room* and *Song of Solomon* and the national awards they received are predicated upon how effectively the two reproduce established and hegemonic literary codes, conventions, themes, and perspectives. The prominent American literary theme of the individual quest for authenticity in a degraded society permeates the tales in *Elbow Room.* Milkman Dead's search in *Song of Solomon* is in the American tradition of Twain's Huck Finn, Faulkner's Quentin, Salinger's Caulfield, James's Isabel, and others. It is their reproduction of dominant themes that allows reviewers and critics to appropriate *Elbow Room* and *Song of Solomon.*

But although critics and reviewers place *Elbow Room* and

Song of Solomon in the American tradition, they also make it
clear that McPherson's stories are "black stories" and that
Morrison's novel is a "black novel." To say that it is "incidental" that McPherson's "stories are about blacks" is to imply that
they are limited, that they have shortcomings. Otherwise, why
the disclaimer? In the late seventies, are these reviewers still
working from a discourse that defines the Afro-American as the
Other and therefore relegates him to a marginal position with an
inferior status in the dominant ideological apparatus? As the inferior, the Afro-American can never be the best. The two are
contradictory terms. Therefore, to be the best, the Afro-
American has to transcend his inferior status and cease being
an Afro-American.

Morrison's *Song of Solomon* is also caught in this double bind:
on the one hand, it is a great novel; on the other it is a black
novel. In the review where she compares *Song of Solomon* to the
works of Faulkner, Heller, Nabokov, and Lessing, Karen DeWitt
of the *Washington Post* calls the novel "Toni Morrison's Saga of
a Black Family." There is an unstated consensus in the American literary establishment that if a novel is great, it cannot be
black. For it to be black, it has to be limited because within the
dominant American ideological apparatus, the Afro-American is
defined as the Other, as different, as inferior.

What we see in post-sixties America is an ideological apparatus that has regained its hegemony at a more sophisticated level.
Its fundamental intellectual categories, "the *specific* aspect of the
concepts of space, time, good, evil, history, causality" have reemerged. Discussing the limitations of the rational group's intellectual categories, Lucien Goldmann contends: "Every group
tends to have an adequate knowledge of reality; but its knowledge can extend only to a maximum horizon compatible with its
existence. Beyond this horizon, information can be received only
if the group's structure is transformed, exactly as in the case of
individual obstacles where information can be received only if
the individual's psychic structure is transformed."[23] The Afro-
American's complex Otherness exists beyond the "maximum horizon" of the dominant American ideological apparatus. The
American ideological apparatus has to repress the Afro-American

complex Other because its presence constitutes a critique: it shows what the American ideological apparatus cannot talk about. For the institutions and practices within the ideological apparatus to receive, to validate the Afro-American's Otherness, they must transform certain structures within their discursive formation, their ideological apparatus. In the sixties, some marginal white groups and individuals began this structural and psychic transformation. But America has never produced the conditions for this group's transformation.

Without the transformation, we find the dominant American ideological apparatus in an interesting bind. On the one hand, it honestly and sincerely wants the Other to be treated justly, to receive all the privileges the society has to offer, but, on the other hand, the only option the ideological apparatus gives the Other is the option to emulate it. The ideological apparatus, because conditions have not dictated, refuses to engage seriously in an examination of those social, political, economic, and intellectual institutions and practices that will accept the Other, that will incorporate the Other into its discursive formation on the Other's own terms.

But just as the institutions and practices of the dominant ideological apparatus in the post-sixties era exclude the Other in Afro-American life, many of the post-sixties Afro-American institutions and practices also exclude within the Afro-American communities. For example, the Rockefeller Foundation Research Fellowship Program for Minority-Group Scholars states that "there are no rigid criteria for eligibility," that there is no discursive selection process in funding proposals from Afro-American scholars. Yet, in examining the mode in which Afro-Americans at the Rockefeller Foundation have funded minority proposals, one finds that they are overwhelmingly positivistic, empirical, and nationalistic. By the nature of its formation, the program, whether intentionally or not, excludes nonempirical and nonpositivistic proposals from Afro-American scholars (such as semiotics, post-structuralism, contemporary Marxism, or hermeneutics). Similar kinds of exclusion of Afro-American research occur in many Afro-American studies programs and departments.

But in excluding the Other in these sixties and seventies Afro-American texts, mainstream reviewers, critics, and normative awarding agencies define them as having the voice of the dominant literary experience. These practices and agencies also make salient the ideological function of normative criticism: to emphasize these texts' effects—the literary conventions and stereotypes they reproduce—that allow them to be appropriated, in order, as Fredric Jameson points out, to "perpetuate only a single voice in this class dialogue, the voice of a hegemonic class."[24]

But some feminist and Afro-American critics—entities that Jameson calls the "non-hegemonic cultural voices"—rewrite the utterances, the interpretations, of mainstream critics, thereby restoring to literary discourse "polemic and subversive strategies" that reaffirm the existence of the Other, the "marginalized or oppositional cultures in our time."[25] If there is a danger, it is whether these Afro-American and feminist critical practices offer alternatives rather than different forms of criticism that define literary texts differently and have different values, beliefs, and goals.

This post-sixties examination of the institutions within the dominant literary establishment shows how these institutions and practices have moved to reestablish control over the Afro-American text and the Afro-American images. Although many Afro-American writers such as Morrison, Walker, Gaines, Murray, McPherson, and others consciously or unconsciously reproduce dominant literary conventions, genres, and stereotypes—thereby allowing their works to be appropriated—the Afro-American in the eighties has not returned to a pre-sixties status, for the restoration of the Afro-American *Other* is clearly established. Many Afro-American studies departments and programs have survived the backlash and are continuing to offer courses and instruction that are *different* from traditional university courses. As discussed above, Afro-American critical practices are reaching levels of sophistication where their voices and interpretations of Afro-American literature have to be acknowledged. Although Afro-American critics such as Houston Baker, Addison Gayle, Robert Stepto, and Barbara Christian, discussed in the first chapter, ignore literary production, they do reject dominant society's assumption about aesthetic beauty to define Afro-

American texts. Afro-American, Native American, Chicano, Asian, and women professors, who understand that normative critical practices are not "natural" but discursive, are revising the American canon. They are including minority and women literature in American literature courses. The Rockefeller Foundation and Ford Foundation are still funding minority scholars and minority-oriented research.

But most important, codified conventions, myths, and stereotypes—be they historical, social, political, literary, or psychological—that dominated much of Afro-American thought for centuries have been exposed and defamiliarized in ways that will never allow them to reestablish their hegemony. The most valuable contribution of the sixties was the de-masking of dominant American society's once universally perceived myths and conventions. And it appears that Afro-American writers, critics, editors, publishing houses are destined, in an almost "natural" or matter-of-fact way, to supersede these myths and conventions, especially the negative, sterile, and debilitating myths about the Afro-American, with themes that signify their own conditions, their own political and cultural concerns and needs. It is this freedom, confidence, and sophistication that make a return to a pre-sixties status an anachronism. These Afro-American, women, and other minority writers, critics, and scholars understand the ideological constraints of the dominant American ideological apparatus. Therefore, they must remain marginal and vocal until the ideological apparatus changes its suppositional base from the single voice of the "hegemonic class" to a pluralistic base that can accommodate all of America's diverse voices.

The impending concerns are: Will these Afro-American, other minorities, and women scholars, writers, and critics interrupt the continual cycle of proliferated authoritarian, absolute critical and literary discourses? Will they engage in their own silences, gaps, exclusions, and oppression? Will they move into a tomorrow where the norm entails an understanding that all discourses are fictions and that if we are going to engage oppression seriously and honestly we must learn to live with these fictions, these Others?

Notes

Chapter 1. Literary Production

1 Pierre Macherey, *A Theory of Literary Production* (London, 1978), p. 16.
2 Terry Eagleton, *Criticism and Ideology* (London, 1976), p. 45.
3 Raymond Williams, *Marxism and Literature* (Oxford, 1977), p. 48.
4 Terry Eagleton, *Literary Theory: An Introduction* (Minneapolis, 1983), p. 11.
5 Eagleton, *Literary Theory,* p. 200.
6 Robert Escarpit, *The Sociology of Literature* (London, 1971), p. 49.
7 Maria Corti, *An Introduction to Literary Semiotics* (Bloomington, Ind., 1978), p. 34.
8 Escarpit, *The Sociology of Literature,* p. 59.
9 Michel Foucault, *The Archaeology of Knowledge* (New York, 1972), p.10.
10 Ibid., p. 38.
11 Houston A. Baker, Jr., "Generational Shifts and the Recent Criticism of Afro-American Literature," *Black American Literature Forum* 15 (Spring 1981): 4.
12 Ibid.
13 Richard Wright, "The Literature of the Negro in the United States," in Addison Gayle, ed., *Black Expression* (New York, 1969), p. 228.
14 Claudia Tate, ed., *Black Women Writers at Work* (New York, 1983), p. 193.
15 Arthur P. Davis, *From the Dark Tower: Afro-American Writers 1900–1960* (Washington, D.C., 1974), p. xiv.
16 Ibid., p. 6.
17 Ibid., p. 139.
18 Ibid., p. 138.
19 Baker, "Generational Shifts," p. 5.
20 Langston Hughes, "The Negro Artist and the Racial Mountain," in Gayle, ed., *Black Expression,* pp. 259–60.
21 LeRoi Jones, *Home: Social Essays* (New York, 1966), p. 110.

22 Robert Stepto, *From Behind the Veil: A Study of Afro-American Narrative* (Urbana, Ill., 1979), p. x.
23 Ibid., p. ix.
24 Ibid.
25 Ibid., pp. ix–x.
26 Ibid., p. x.
27 Houston A. Baker, Jr., *The Journey Back: Issues in Black Literature and Criticism* (Chicago, 1980), p. xii.
28 Ibid., p. 1.
29 Edward Sapir, *Selected Writings in Language, Culture, and Personality* (Berkeley, 1949), p. 162.
30 Baker, *The Journey Back,* p. 19.
31 Barbara Christian, *Black Women Novelists: The Development of a Tradition, 1892–1976* (Westport, Conn., 1980), p. x.
32 Ibid., p. x.
33 Ibid.
34 Ibid., p. 5.
35 Ibid., pp. 239, 240.
36 Ibid., p. xi.
37 Eagleton, *Criticism and Ideology,* p. 48.
38 Christian, *Black Women Novelists,* p. 41.

Chapter 2. The Dominant Literary Establishment

1 James Baldwin, *Black Man In America* (Album), Credo IA, An Interview by Studs Terkel, Produced by Joe Berk (Cambridge, Mass.)
2 Roland Barthes, *Mythologies* (New York, 1972), pp. 151–52.
3 Sylvia Wynter, "History, Ideology, and the Reinvention of the Past in Achebe's *Things Fall Apart* and Laye's *The Dark Child,*" *Minority Voices* 2 (1978): 44.
4 Lucy Tompkins, "In the Florida Glades," *New York Times Book Review* (September 26, 1937), p. 29.
5 George Stevens, "Negroes by Themselves," *Saturday Review of Literature* (September 18, 1937), p. 3.
6 Ibid.
7 "Negropings," *Time* (September 20, 1937), p. 71.
8 Richard Wright, "Between Laughter and Tears," *New Masses* (October 5, 1937), pp. 23, 25.
9 Robert F. Moss, "The Arts in Black America," *Saturday Review* (November 15, 1975), p. 16.
10 Alain Locke, "Reason and Race," *Phylon* (March–June 1947): 18.
11 Arna Bontemps, "Books," *New York Herald Tribune Weekly Book Review* (February 10, 1964), p. 4.
12 Henry Tracy, "Books," *Common Ground* (Summer 1946): 106.

13 Alfred Butterfield, "The Dark Heartbeat of Harlem," *New York Times Book Review* (February 10, 1946), p. 6.

14 Malcolm Cowley, "The Case of Bigger Thomas," *New Republic* (March 18, 1940), p. 382.

15 Peter Monro Jack, "A Tragic Novel of Negro Life in America," *New York Times Book Review* (March 3, 1940), p. 2.

16 Jonathan Daniels, "Man Against the World," *Nation* (March 2, 1940), p. 5.

17 Robert M Farnsworth, introduction to Charles Chesnutt, *The Marrow of Tradition* (Ann Arbor, 1969), p. v.

18 Darwin Turner, introduction to Charles W. Chesnutt, *The House Behind the Cedars* (London, 1969), p. xiii.

19 Ibid.

20 Ibid., pp. xiii, xiv.

21 Charles Chesnutt, letter to Mr. Cable, June 5, 1890, Charles Chesnutt Collection, Fisk University Library, Nashville, Tennessee.

22 Farnsworth, introduction to Chesnutt, *The Marrow of Tradition,* p. xvi.

23 Addison Gayle, *The Way of the New World* (Garden City, N.Y., 1975), p. 44.

24 Nathan Irvin Huggins, *Harlem Renaissance* (New York, 1971), p. 7.

25 Ibid., p. 84.

26 Darwin T. Turner, *In A Minor Chord: Three Afro-American Writers and Their Search for Identity* (Carbondale, Ill., 1971), p. 2.

27 Darwin T. Turner, introduction to Jean Toomer, *Cane* (New York, 1975), p. ix.

28 Ibid.

29 Darwin T. Turner, ed., *The Wayward and the Seeking: A Collection of Writings by Jean Toomer* (Washington, D.C., 1982), p. 1.

30 Huggins, *Harlem Renaissance,* p. 118.

31 Langston Hughes, *The Big Sea: An Autobiography* (New York, 1940), p. 316.

32 Ibid., p. 323.

33 Huggins, *Harlem Renaissance,* p. 128.

34 Hughes, *The Big Sea,* pp. 238–39.

35 Ibid., p. 325.

36 Ernest Jones, *Nation* (February 11, 1950), p. 139.

37 Harvey Webster, *Saturday Review of Literature* (April 12, 1952), p. 22.

38 Wright Morris, *New York Times Book Review* (April 13, 1952), p. 5.

39 "Black and Blue," *Time* (April 14, 1952), p. 112.

Chapter 3. Sixties' Social Movements

1 Paul A. Baran and Paul M. Sweezy, *Monopoly Capital* (New York, 1966), p. 267.

2 Jürgen Habermas, *Legitimation Crisis* (Boston, 1973), p. 46.

3 Ibid., p. 48.

4 Louis Kampf and Paul Lauter, eds., *The Politics of Literature: Dissenting Essays on the Teaching of English* (New York, 1972), p. 8.

5 Richard Goldstein, "The War for America's Mind," *Village Voice* 27 (1982): 11.

6 Ishmael Reed, *Mumbo Jumbo* (Garden City, N.Y., 1973), p. 10.

7 Ibid., p. 12.
8 Fredric Jameson, *The Political Unconscious: Narrative as a Socially Symbolic Act* (Ithaca, 1981), p. 86.
9 John O'Brien, ed., *Interview with Black Writers* (New York, 1973), pp. 82–83.
10 Robert Stepto, "Study and Experience: An Interview with Ralph Ellison," *Massachusetts Review* 18 (Autumn 1977): 430.
11 James Alan McPherson, "On Becoming an American Writer," *Atlantic Monthly* (December 1978): 57.
12 Pat Crutchfield Exum, introduction to Pat C. Exum, ed., *Keeping the Faith* (New York, 1974), p. 13.
13 Talk of the Town, "Ntozake Shange," *New Yorker* (August 2, 1976), p. 18.
14 Alice Walker, "One Child of One's Own," *Ms.* (August 1979), p. 75.
15 Terry Eagleton, *Literary Theory: An Introduction* (Minneapolis, 1983), p. 11.

Chapter 4. The Black Nationalist Discourse

1 John O'Brien, ed., *Interviews with Black Writers* (New York, 1973), pp. 82–83.
2 Ibid.
3 Ruth Laney, "A Conversation with Ernest Gaines," *Southern Review* 10 (January 1974): 2.
4 Alphonso Pinkney, *Red, Black and Green: Black Nationalism in the United States* (New York, 1976), p. 6.
5 Amiri Baraka, *Raise, Race, Rays, Rage* (New York, 1971), p. 89.
6 Eric Foner, "In Search of Black History," *New York Review of Books* (October 22, 1970), p. 11.
7 Ernest J. Gaines, *The Autobiography of Miss Jane Pittman* (New York, 1971), p. vii. (All quotes are taken from the Bantam edition.)
8 Ibid., pp. v–vi.
9 Georg Lukács, "Idea and Form in Literature," in *Marxism and Human Liberation* (New York, 1973), pp. 118–19.
10 Gaines, *The Autobiography of Miss Jane Pittman*, p. 11.
11 Ibid., p. 41.
12 Ibid., p. 44.
13 Ibid., p. 16.
14 Ibid., p. 95.
15 Jerry H. Bryant, "From Life to Death: The Function of Ernest J. Gaines," *Iowa Review* 3 (Winter, 1972): 117.
16 William L. Andrews, "The Idea of Progress," *Black American Literature Forum* 2 (Winter 1977): 147.
17 Gaines, *The Autobiography of Miss Jane Pittman*, p. 145.
18 Ibid., p. 146.
19 Ibid., p. 173.
20 Ibid., p. 193.
21 James R. Giles, "Revolution and Myth: Kelley's *A Different Drummer* and Gaines's *The Autobiography of Miss Jane Pittman,*" *Minority Voices* 1 (Fall 1977): 47.

22 Gaines, *The Autobiography of Miss Jane Pittman,* p. 216.
23 Ibid., p. 101.
24 Ibid., pp. 200, 203, 204.
25 Ibid., pp. 224–25.
26 Ibid., p. 228.
27 Ibid., p. 246.
28 O'Brien, ed., *Interviews with Black Writers,* p. 85.
29 Paule Marshall, "Characterizations of Black Women in The American Novel," in Juliette Bowles, ed., *In the Memory and Spirit of Frances, Zora, and Lorraine* (Washington, D.C., 1979), p. 78.
30 The blues idiom paradigm allows for life in all its possibilities, limitations, potentialities, and absurdities. It allows for the entire spectrum of the human existence. See Albert Murray, *The Omni-Americans* (New York, 1970).
31 Jerry H. Bryant, "Ernest J. Gaines: Change, Growth, and History," *Southern Review* 10 (October 1974): 851; "Politics and the Black Novel," *The Nation* 212 (April 5, 1971): 437.
32 Geoffrey Wolff, "Talking to Trees," *Newsweek* (May 3, 1971), p. 103.
33 Giles, "Revolution and Myth," p. 39.
34 Addison Gayle, *The Way of the New World: The Black Novel in America* (New York, 1975), p. 294.
35 Arthenia Bates Millican, "Review of *The Autobiography of Miss Jane Pittman,*" *CLA Journal* (September 1971): 96.

Chapter 5. The Feminist Discourse

1 Fredric Jameson, *The Political Unconscious* (Ithaca, 1981), p. 79.
2 John O'Brien, ed., *Interviews with Black Writers* (New York, 1973), pp. 192, 196–197.
3 Jameson, *The Political Unconscious,* p. 87.
4 M. M. Bakhtin, *The Dialogic Imagination* (Austin, 1981), p. 262.
5 Alice Walker, *The Third Life of Grange Copeland* (New York, 1970), p. 5.
6 Ibid.
7 Ibid., p. 8.
8 Ibid.
9 Ibid., p. 10.
10 Ibid., pp. 11–13.
11 Mary Helen Washington, "Black Women Image Makers," *Black World* (August 1974): 13.
12 Ibid.
13 See Julia Kristeva, *Desire in Language* (New York, 1980), for further examination of this subject. Also see Jameson, *The Political Unconscious.*
14 Walker, *The Third Life of Grange Copeland,* pp. 40–41.
15 Ibid., pp. 38–39.
16 Ibid., p. 54.

17 Ibid., pp. 54–55.
18 Ibid., p. 153.
19 Ibid., pp. 155, 196, 198.
20 Ibid., p. 214.
21 Jameson, *The Political Unconcious,* p. 79.
22 Walker, *The Third Life of Grange Copeland,* p. 5.
23 Ibid., p. 42.
24 Ibid., p. 136.
25 Pierre Macherey, *A Theory of Literary Production* (London, 1968), pp. 79–80.
26 Walker, *The Third Life of Grange Copeland,* pp. 94, 96.
27 Ibid., 95.
28 Ibid., p. 206.
29 Michel Foucault, *The Archaeology of Knowledge* (New York, 1972), p. 44.
30 Trudier Harris, "Violence in *The Third Life of Grange Copeland,*" *CLA Journal* (December 1975): 246.
31 Walker, *The Third Life of Grange Copeland,* p. 58.
32 David Bradley, "Telling the Black Woman's Story," *New York Times Magazine* (January 8, 1984), p. 36.

Chapter 6. The Blues Idiom Style

1 Albert Murray, *The Omni-Americans* (New York, 1970), pp. 88–90, and *The Hero and the Blues* (Columbia, 1973), p. 37.
2 Murray, *The Omni-Americans,* pp. 19–20.
3 Murray, *The Hero and the Blues,* p. 44.
4 Murray, *The Omni-Americans,* pp. 14–15, and *The Hero and the Blues,* p. 5.
5 Ibid., p. 15.
6 John Wideman, "Luzana Cholly and the Citizens of Gasoline Point," *New York Times Book Review* (May 12, 1974), p. 7.
7 We can take this statement as a signal that Murray intends to speak generally and categorically about Afro-American life in the 1920s.
8 Albert Murray, *Train Whistle Guitar* (New York, 1974), pp. 1, 3.
9 Ibid., p. 4.
10 Ibid.
11 Ibid., p. 14.
12 Ibid., pp. 13, 14.
13 Ibid., p. 8.
14 Ibid., pp. 31–32.
15 Ibid., p. 32.
16 Ibid., p. 34.
17 Ibid., p. 36.
18 Ibid.
19 Ibid., p. 107.
20 James Alan McPherson, "The View from the Chinaberry Tree," *Atlantic Monthly* (December 1974), p. 121.

21 Murray, *Train Whistle Guitar*, p. 64.

22 Ibid., pp. 68–69.

23 Ibid., pp. 56–57.

24 Ibid., pp. 48–49.

25 Ibid., p. 63.

26 Ibid., p. 92.

27 Ibid., pp. 94–95.

28 Ibid., p. 96.

29 Ibid., p. 103.

30 Ibid., p. 122.

31 Ibid., pp. 106–7.

32 Ibid., p. 108.

33 Murray, *The Omni-Americans*, p. 31.

34 Murray, *Train Whistle Guitar*, p. 82.

35 McPherson, "The View from the Chinaberry Tree," p. 120.

36 Murray, *Train Whistle Guitar*, pp. 72–73.

37 Terry Eagleton, *Criticism and Ideology* (London, 1976), p. 74.

38 Murray, *The Hero and the Blues*, p. 39.

39 Murray, *The Omni-Americans*, pp. 214, 217.

40 Murray, *The Hero and the Blues*, p. 38.

41 Dorothy Gillian, "The Riff-Style Intellectual," *Washington Post* (June 6, 1974), sec. B, p. 3.

Chapter 7. The Production of the Historical Past

1 Ntozake Shange, "Interview with Toni Morrison," *American Rag* 2 (Fall 1978): 48.

2 Colette Dowling, "The Song of Toni Morrison," *New York Times Magazine* (May 20, 1979), p. 56.

3 Diane Johnson, "The Oppressor in the Next Room," *New York Review of Books* (November 10, 1977), p. 6.

4 Pepsi Charles, "An Interview with Toni Morrison," *Nimrod* 21–22 (1977): 43.

5 Dowling, "The Song of Toni Morrison," p. 58.

6 Paula Giddings, "The Triumphant Song of Toni Morrison," *Encore American & Worldwide News* (December 12, 1977), p. 30.

7 Bettye J. Parker, "Complexity: Toni Morrison's Women—An Interview Essay," in Bell, Parker, and Guy-Scheffall, eds., *Sturdy Black Bridges: Visions of Black Women in Literature* (Garden City, N.Y., 1979), pp. 252–53.

8 Dorothy Gillian, "The Black Book: How It Was Made," *Washington Post* (March 6, 1974), sec. B. p. 1.

9 Toni Morrison, "Rediscovering Black History," *New York Times Magazine* (August 11, 1974), p. 14.

10 In the interview with Ntozake Shange, Morrsion argues that because her generation was overly preoccupied with becoming middle class and acquiring the approval of the dominant society, it forgot to pass on to its children, the

succeeding generations, those values and "truths" that were crucial in the survival of black people in America. See Shange, "Interview with Toni Morrison."

11 Robert B. Stepto, "Intimate Things in Place: A Conversation with Toni Morrison," *Massachusetts Review* 18 (Autumn 1977): 474.

12 Toni Morrison, "To Be a Black Woman," *New York Times Book Review* (March 28, 1971), p. 3.

13 Giddings, "The Triumphant Song of Toni Morrison," p. 30.

14 Charles, "An Interview with Toni Morrison," p. 44.

15 Giddings, "The Triumphant Song of Toni Morrison,", p. 30.

16 Dowling, "The Song of Toni Morrison," p. 56.

17 Toni Morrison, *Sula* (New York, 1974), p. 3.

18 Ibid., p. 4.

19 Ibid., p. 6.

20 Ibid., p. 12.

21 Ibid., p. 14.

22 Ibid., pp. 14–15.

23 Ibid., p. 15.

24 Michel Foucault, *Madness and Civilization: A History of Insanity in the Age of Reason* (New York, 1965), p. ix.

25 Morrison, *Sula,* pp. 15, 16.

26 Claude Lévi-Strauss, *The Savage Mind* (Chicago, 1966), pp. 16–17.

27 Ibid., pp. 17, 21–22, 93.

28 Morrison, *Sula,* p. 18.

29 Barbara Christian, *Black Women Novelists: The Development of a Tradition, 1892–1976* (Westport, Conn., 1980), p. 158.

30 Morrison, *Sula,* p. 32.

31 Claudia Tate (ed.), *Black Women Writers at Work* (New York, 1983), p. 123.

32 Morrison, *Sula,* p. 40.

33 Foucault, *Madness and Civilization,* pp. 16–17.

34 Morrison, *Sula,* p. 44.

35 Ibid., p. 42.

36 Ibid., pp. 89–90.

37 Ibid., pp. 117–18.

38 Ibid., p. 153.

39 Ibid., p. 166.

40 Shange, "Interview with Toni Morrison," p. 50.

41 Morrison, *Sula,* p. 164.

42 Ibid., p. 30.

43 Ibid., pp. 68, 69.

44 Ibid., p. 36.

45 Ibid., pp. 120–21.

46 Cathleen Medwick, "People Are Talking About . . ." *Vogue* (April 1981): 289.

47 Morrison, *Sula,* p. 32.

48 Ibid., p. 49.

49 Ibid., p. 52.
50 Ibid., p. 174.

Chapter 8. The Post-Sixties

1 Harry Magdoff and Paul M. Sweezy, *The End of Prosperity: The American Economy in the 1970s* (New York, 1977), p. vii.
2 Ibid., p. viii.
3 Richard Goldstein, "The War for America's Mind," *Village Voice* 27 (1982): 12.
4 Ibid., p. 11.
5 What is particuarly interesting about these these new humanities core courses is that they need the participation of the Other, the oppositional voices—women and minorities—to legitimate their existence.
6 David Bradley, "Black and American, 1982," *Esquire* (May 1982), p. 69.
7 June Jordan, *Civil Wars* (Boston, 1981), p. 163.
8 Guy Debord, *Society of the Spectacle* (Detroit, 1970), p. 1.
9 Loyle Hairston, "Work of Rare Beauty and Power," *Freedomways* 2 (1971): 171.
10 Robert Coles, "Try Men's Souls," *New Yorker* (February 27, 1971), p. 104.
11 Mark Schorer, "Novels and Nothingness," *American Scholar* 40 (Winter, 1970–71): 172.
12 See Trudier Harris, "Violence in *The Third Life of Grange Copeland*," *CLA Journal* (December 1975): p. 246.
13 Claudia Tate, ed., *Black Women Writers at Work* (New York, 1983), pp. 76–77.
14 David Bradley, "Telling The Black Woman's Story," *New York Times Magazine* (January 8, 1984), pp. 28–29.
15 Thomas P. Edwards, "Can You Go Home Again?" *New York Review of Books* (June 13, 1974), p. 38.
16 "Books," *New Yorker* (July 22, 1974), p. 83.
17 Celia Betsky, "Center of Black Universe," *Washington Post* (April 20, 1974), sec. 3. p. 5.
18 Barbara Christian, *Black Women Novelists: The Development of a Tradition, 1892-1976* (Westport, Conn., 1980), p. 153.
19 "Notes by the Editors," *The Antioch Review* 36 (Winter 1978): 130.
20 Ray Walters, "Paperback Talk," *New York Times Book Review* (September 2, 1979), p. 17.
21 Diane Johnson, "The Oppressor in the Next Room," *New York Review of Books* (November 10, 1977), p. 7.
22 John Leonard, "To Ride the Air to Africa," *New York Times* (September 6, 1977), p. 3.
23 Lucien Goldmann, *Cultural Creation* (St Louis, 1976), pp. 34, 35.
24 Fredric Jameson, *The Political Unconscious: Narrative as a Socially Symbolic Act* (Ithaca, 1981), p. 85.
25 Ibid., p. 86.

Bibliography

Note: A full bibliography of modern linguistics, structuralism, semiotics, and poststructuralism would require a volume by itself. The following is a list of books that I found useful for this study.

Althusser, Louis. *Lenin and Philosophy and Other Essays.* Translated by Ben Brewster. London, 1971.

Baker, Houston A., Jr. *The Journey Back: Issues in Black Literature and Criticism.* Chicago, 1980.

Bakhtin, M. M. *The Dialogic Imagination.* Austin, 1981.

Barthes, Roland. *Images, Music, Text.* Translated by Stephen Heath. New York, 1977.

———. *S/Z.* New York, 1974.

———. *The Pleasure of the Text.* Translated by Richard Miller. New York, 1975.

———. *Elements of Semiology.* Translated by Annette Lavers and Colin Smith. New York, 1968.

Barthold, Bonnie J. *Black Time: Fiction of Africa, the Carribbean, and the United States.* New Haven, 1981.

Bellamy, Joe David. *The New Fiction: Interviews With Innovative American Writers.* Urbana, Ill., 1974.

Bennett, Tony. *Formalism and Marxism.* New York, 1974.

Berthoff, Warner. *A Literature Without Qualities: American Writing Since 1945.* Berkeley, 1979.

Brinton, Crane, ed. *The Portable Age of Reason Reader.* New York, 1956.

Burns, Tom, and Elizabeth Burns, eds. *Sociology of Literature and Drama.* Middlesex, 1973.

Christian, Barbara. *Black Women Novelists: The Development of a Tradition, 1892–1976.* Westport, Conn., 1980.

Corti, Maria. *An Introduction to Literary Semiotics*. Translated by M. Bogat and
    A. Mandelbaum. Bloomington, Ind., 1978.
Coward, Rosalind, and John Ellis. *Language and Materialism: Development in
    Semiology and the Theory of the Subject*. London, 1979.
Culler, Jonathan. *Structuralist Poetics: Structuralism, Linguistics, and the Study of
    Literature*. Ithaca, 1975.
De George, Richard, and Fernande De George, eds. *The Structuralists*. New
    York, 1972.
Dickstein, Morris. *Gates of Eden: American Culture in the Sixties*. New York, 1977.
Durant, Will, and Ariel Durant. *The Age of Reason Begins*. New York, 1961.
Eagleton, Terry. *Criticism and Ideology*. London, 1976.
_____. *Literary Theory: An Introduction*. Minneapolis, 1983.
_____. *Marxism and Literary Criticism*. Berkeley, 1976.
Eco, Umberto. *A Theory of Semiotics*. Bloomington, Ind., 1976.
_____. *The Role of the Reader*. Bloomington, Ind., 1979.
Exum, Pat Crutchfield, ed. *Keeping The Faith*. New York, 1974.
Federman, Raymond, ed. *Surfiction: Fiction Now. . .And Tomorrow*. Chicago, 1975.
Foucault, Michel. *Madness and Civilization: A History of Insanity in the Age of
    Reason*. New York, 1966.
_____. *The Archaeology of Knowledge and the Discourse on Language*.
    Translated by Sheridan Smith. New York, 1976.
_____. *Discipline and Punish: The Birth of the Prison*. New York, 1977.
_____. *Language, Counter-Memory, Practice*. Oxford, 1977.
_____. *Power/Knowledge: Selected Interviews and Other Writings, 1972–1977*.
    New York, 1980.
Gayle, Addison, ed. *The Black Aesthetic*. Garden City, N.Y., 1972.
_____. *The Way of The New World: The Black Novel in America*. Garden City,
    N.Y., 1975.
_____. *Black Expression*. New York, 1969.
Geertz, Clifford. *The Interpretation of Cultures*. New York, 1974.
Gellner, Ernest. *Legitimation of Belief*. London, 1974.
Goldmann, Lucien. *Essays On Method in the Sociology of Literature*. St. Louis, 1980.
_____. *Cultural Creation*. St Louis, 1976.
_____. *Towards a Sociology of the Novel*. London, 1975.
Habermas, Jürgen. *Toward a Rational Society*. Boston, 1970.
_____. *Legitimation Crisis*. Boston, 1973.
Harari, Josue, ed. *Textual Strategies: Perspectives in Post-Structuralist Criticism*.
    Ithaca, 1979.
Hawkes, Terence. *Structuralism and Semiotics*. Berkeley, 1977.
Heimann, Edward. *Reason and Faith in Modern Society: Liberalism, Marxism,
    and Democracy*. Middletown, Conn., 1961.
Huggins, Nathan. *Harlem Renaissance*. New York, 1971.
Hughes, Langston. *The Big Sea: An Autobiography*. New York, 1940.
Iser, Wolfgang. *The Act of Reading: A Theory of Aesthetic Response*. Baltimore, 1978.

——. *The Implied Reader: Patterns of Communication in Prose Fiction from Bunyan to Beckett.* Baltimore, 1976.

Jakobson, Roman. *Selected Writings.* The Hague, 1979.

Jameson, Fredric. *The Prison House of Language: A Critical Account of Structuralism and Russian Formalism.* Princeton, 1970.

——. *Marxism and Form.* Princeton, 1971.

——. *The Political Unconscious: Narrative as a Socially Symbolic Act.* Ithaca, 1981.

Jones, LeRoi, and Larry Neal, eds. *Black Fire: An Anthology of Afro-American Writing.* New York, 1968.

——. *Home: Social Essays.* New York, 1966.

Jordan, June. *Civil Wars.* Boston, 1981.

Kent, George. *Blackness and The Adventure of Western Culture.* Chicago, 1972.

Kristeva, Julia. *Desire in Language: A Semiotic Approach to Literature and Art.* New York, 1980.

Kress, Gunther, and Robert Hodge. *Language as Ideology.* Boston, 1981.

Kuhn, Thomas S. *The Structure of Scientific Revolutions.* Chicago, 1970.

Lacan, Jacques. *The Language of the Self.* New York, 1975.

Lane, Michael, ed. *Structuralism: A Reader.* London, 1970.

Lentricchia, Frank. *After the New Criticism.* Chicago, 1980.

Lévi-Strauss, Claude. *The Savage Mind.* Chicago, 1966.

——. *Structural Anthropology.* New York, 1963.

Lovell, Terry. *Pictures of Reality: Aesthetics, Politics, and Pleasure.* London, 1980.

Lukács, Georg. *History and Class Consciousness.* Cambridge, Mass., 1971.

——. *The Theory of the Novel.* Translated by Anna Bostock. Cambridge, Mass., 1971.

——. *Realism in Our Time: Literature and the Class Struggle.* New York, 1971.

Macherey, Pierre. *A Theory of Literary Production.* London, 1978.

Macksey, Richard, and Eugenio Donato, eds. *The Structuralist Controversy.* Baltimore, 1970.

Marcuse, Herbert. *Reason and Revolution: Hegel and the Rise of Social Theory.* New York, 1954.

Mayntz, Renate, Kurt Holm, and Roger Huebner. *Introduction to Empirical Sociology.* Middlesex, 1969.

Morris, Meaghan, and Paul Patton. *Michel Foucault: Power, Truth, Strategy.* Sydney, 1979.

Murray, Albert. *South to a Very Old Place.* New York, 1971.

——. *The Omni-Americans.* New York, 1970.

——. *The Hero and the Blues.* Columbia, Mo., 1973.

O'Brien, John, ed. *Interviews with Black Writers.* New York, 1973.

Penner, Dick. *Fiction of the Absurd.* New York, 1980

Pettit, Philip. *The Concept of Structuralism: A Critical Analysis.* Berkeley, 1975.

Piaget, Jean. *Structuralism.* New York, 1970.

Pinkney, Alphonso. *Red, Black, and Green: Black Nationalism in the United States.* New York, 1976.

Said, Edward W. *Beginnings: Intention and Method.* Baltimore, 1975.

———. *Orientalism.* New York, 1978.

Sammons, Jeffrey L. *Literary Sociology and Practical Criticism: An Inquiry.* Bloomington, Ind., 1977.

Sapir, Edward. *Selected Writings in Language, Culture, and Personality.* Berkeley, 1949.

Sartre, Jean-Paul. *Being and Nothingness.* Translated by Hazel E. Barnes. New York, 1956.

Saussure, Ferdinand de. *Course in General Linguistics.* New York, 1966.

Schiller, Herbert I. *Communication and Cultural Domination.* White Plains, N.Y., 1976.

Scholes, Robert. *Structuralism in Literature.* New Haven, 1974.

Schramm, Wilbur Lang, and Donald Roberts. *The Process and Effects of Mass Communication.* Urbana, Ill., 1971.

Smith, Barbara Herrnstein. *On the Margins of Discourse: The Relation of Literature to Language.* Chicago, 1978.

Stepto, Robert. *From Behind the Veil: A Study of Afro-American Narrative.* Urbana, Ill., 1979.

Sumner, Colin. *Reading Ideologies: An Investigation into the Marxist Theory of Ideology and Law.* New York, 1979.

Snyder, Louis L. *The Age of Reason.* New York, 1955.

Tate, Claudia, ed. *Black Women Writers at Work.* New York, 1983.

Turner, Darwin T. *In a Minor Chord: Three Afro-American Writers and Their Search for Identity.* Carbondale, Ill., 1971.

———, ed. *The Wayward and the Seeking: A Collection of Writings by Jean Toomer.* Washington, D.C., 1982.

Walcutt, Charles Child. *American Literary Naturalism: A Divided Stream.* Minneapolis, 1956.

Weinstein, Leo, ed. *The Age of Reason.* New York, 1965.

Williams, Raymond. *Culture and a Society, 1780–1950.* Edinburgh, 1961.

———. *The Sociology of Culture.* New York, 1982.

Index

W. Lawrence Hogue is Assistant Professor, Department of English and Comparative Literature, University of California at Irvine.